JOURNEY TO PROSPERITY

WRITTEN AND PHOTOGRAPHED BY G. ALAN SIEVE

A cruise ship heads up the Inside Passage to Juneau, Alaska.

TABLE OF CONTENTS

My mother reflects upon her family's homestead in Canada.

Follow the pioneers

Self-reliance is a key to wealth building

I've never had a high salary. In my best year, I made $35,000 as an editor in chief, supervising a staff of six working on three weekly newspapers, in which I was part owner. At the time I retired in October 2012, I was making $26,500 after eight and one-half years as a copy editor/page designer on a small-to-medium-sized daily.

Yet, I have a great lifestyle; I have no debt on my home — an all-brick condominium, which the property tax assessor values at $304,100, I own two classic Ford Mustang collectible cars that are paid for, and I have a sizable net worth.

> *"As I get older, I pay less attention to what men say. I just look at what they do."*
> — ANDREW CARNEGIE

How did I do it? Or, more importantly, how can you do it? That's the subject of this book.

My three keys to success are:
• Live well, beneath your means.
• Start to save as soon as you can and save as much as you for as long as you can.
• Invest wisely.

I know all that's easier said than done, but through this book, I'll go into those in detail, citing research to back up my own personal experience and providing you with practical steps you can follow on your own journey to prosperity.

However, this is not a how-to manual. There are other sources for that. Rather, I hope to inspire you to change your mindset, which will enable you to pursue your own measure of success.

And through the photographs and quotations that accompany this text, I hope to engage you not only on an intellectual level but also on emotional and spiritual levels.

This is about changing your life. By embracing these ideas on multiple levels, you'll greatly enhance your chances of success.

I acquired a self-reliant mindset from my parents, especially my mother, whose family was among the last of the pioneers.

I dedicate this book to her because she always espoused pulling yourself up by your bootstraps, and she had wanted to write a book telling how she had learned to do so. As the journalist in the family, I will take up that challenge in her honor.

Homesteading in Canada

In 1906, when my mother was 3, her family homesteaded in western Saskatchewan, Canada, about 40 miles east of the Saskatchewan/Alberta border.

She insisted they were the first to settle in what is now Mariposa (rural municipality No. 350).

They lived in a tent until they finished a sod house, a cabin built with prairie sod. Over the next few years, they would build another 'soddy' before eventually settling into a two-story frame house.

It was determination and hard work that enabled them to survive and even thrive on the Canadian frontier.

After living in two sod houses, my mother's family built this frame house, which was being used as a granary when we visited in 1978.

She always stressed that kind of self-reliance, as well as faith in God, as the ways to succeed in life.

She regaled my sisters, my brother and I with stories of life on the plains: how her father plowed furrows around their house with a horse-drawn harrow to create a firebreak while a growing prairie fire approached, how they had to cut steps into snowdrifts to go outside their front door during the Canadian winter, and how she and her siblings walked or rode horses to school in the nearby settlement of Broadacres.

Ironically, rather than exaggerating that distance like many elders reportedly do, my mother insisted they lived just outside town.

It wasn't until we visited in 1978, and drove the distance, that we discovered—to her surprise—that it was five miles.

The family lived there until 1918, when they decided to return to western Iowa.

Being the children of German immigrants living in a British country during World War I—and having an outspoken anti-British relative living nearby—these American citizens decided it was time to move back home to Breda, Iowa.

Living through the Great Depression

After finishing eighth grade (few of her generation went to high school) my mother worked as a housekeeper for a small-town banker until she married my father in 1925.

They started their life together renting a hardscrabble farm in southern Iowa. This is where they weathered the Great Depression.

She told us how they had to patch holes in the foundation of the old farmhouse to keep rats out.

They didn't wait for the owner to do it, and they were subsequently praised by him for how well they kept up the property.

You shouldn't wait for someone else to fix your problems; you should do so yourself.

— JULIA SIEVE, MY MOTHER

Her moral to that story was that **you shouldn't wait for someone else to fix your problems; you should do so yourself**.

They returned to Western Iowa in the 1940s so my father could help my grandfather farm their home place, which he did until my grandfather died.

Following my grandfather's death, my father decided to leave farming — the only life he'd known.

He worked on the railroad for a short time. Then he settled into a job as a gas station attendant.

He apparently liked it—or was at least satisfied with it.

He stayed at it until his death in 1969 at age 73.

A life of contentment

They built a small home (a typical post-World War II cracker box) in Carroll, Iowa, where I grew up, and where my mother—in her typical pull-yourself-up-by-your-own-bootstraps fashion (and against my father's objections that a wife shouldn't work outside the home)—went to work as a salesclerk in a fabric and women's wear store, where she stayed until age 84.

She noted that her working enabled our family to afford more than we could have otherwise.

In high school, I was surprised to learn through textbooks that, based on our household income, we were considered "working poor" by socio-economists.

I never felt that we were poor.

But my parents seemed content.

We always had enough to eat, we always had decent clothes, and my dad even bought a new car every couple of years.

Although I never got everything I wanted, I learned to get creative through drawing and making a lot of my own toys with cardboard and scraps of wood. Creativity is probably one of the best gifts a child can receive.

And upon her death in 1998, my mother left her four children a paid-for house and a $120,000 estate—not bad for her time.

Like her, I believe adopting the values she espoused and time-honored financial practices can help anyone achieve their own American Dream—not necessarily the big house-with-two-cars-in-the-garage view of suburbia cited by its critics—but to achieve one's own goals, whatever they are.

My challenges were different

Like everyone else, I've had my ups and downs along my way to prosperity, which were different from hers.

Due to a birth injury, I have slight paralysis to one side of my face, a slow and slightly awkward gait, and a speech impediment that are obvious handicaps and, unfortunately, people do judge a book by its cover.

I know it hurt me as I sought a social life and career and tried to climb the ladder of my own success.

But I was also the first in my family to go to college (at a young age I recall being told I would need to go to college because I couldn't get a "regular" job; my mother later insisted that she never said that).

Rather than acquiring a pioneering spirit like my mother's, I acquired an entrepreneurial spirit, which is perhaps the same thing.

After being laid off from my first job, I was unemployed for a year, then started a career in journalism, joining a weekly newspaper group as a reporter-photographer.

I became editor of one of the weeklies, bought into the company, earned a master's degree in journalism at the University of Missouri-Columbia, and became editor in chief of three of our newspapers.

By 2000, newspapers were selling for premium prices, so we sold our small but successful chain to *The Des Moines Register*, which was owned by Gannett, then one of the nation's largest media companies.

I felt I had outgrown the weekly newspaper field, and I longed for a fuller life so I took my share of the money and ran, settling in the foothills of East Tennessee between Knoxville and Great Smoky Mountains National Park.

Since then, my investments declined three

A broken down wagon—not my grandparents'—rested behind the house.

times: once after 9/11 and the dot-com bust, again—this time by more than 40 percent— in the stock market crash of 2008–2009, and most recently in the aftermath of the 2020 pandemic.

But after each of those experiences, my investments recovered as my advisor had assured me that they would.

I achieved my retirement goal, not by age 65 as I'd hoped but by age 67. Like my parents, I am content.

And if you follow the time-tested principles on the pages that follow, I am confident you too can achieve your own success.

If we could do it, you can too.

Day breaks over the Great Smoky Mountains along Foothills Parkway in East Tennessee.

"It is well to be up before daybreak, for such habits contribute to health, wealth and wisdom."

— ARISTOTLE

CHAPTER 1

You too can become financially successful

The majority of millionaires grew their wealth over the course of their lifetimes

As noted before, I never earned a large salary.

Because I believed I might never do so, I came to the realization as a young man that if I wanted to have enough money to buy a nice home, to buy fine cars and to have a comfortable retirement, I was going to have to save on the routine, everyday expenses of life, just like my mother and father had done when they started out.

Also in my mid-20s, while working at my first job after college, I heard the financial advice that to grow enough wealth for a comfortable retirement, you should save 10 percent of your income each year.

Without any further thought about how I'd do it, I said to myself, "I want to be ahead of the curve; I'm going to **save 20 percent**."

And, having learned frugality from my mother, I set about trying to do just that.

Toward the end of that decade, I also read that those people who **set a specific goal**, such as earning $1 million by age 65, rather than just saying they wanted to retire rich, stood a much better chance of achieving that goal.

And those that actually set out the small steps they were going to take to reach their large goal stood the best chance of all of achieving it.

Then, in 1980—I was 30 at the time—interest rates spiked to near 20 percent on my money market fund, and banks were advertising that one could save $1 million over 40 years by saving

Follow these 10 steps to achieve financial prosperity

1. Live well, beneath your means: Look for ways to save money on everyday expenses. This will give you more money to save for what you really want, to pay off debt and to save for the future.

2. Start an emergency fund: Begin by saving $1,000 to $2,000. That should cover most minor emergencies like a broken limb or fixing your car so you have transportation to get to work.

3. Get your employer's match: Invest enough in your retirement plan at work to get any match offered. That's usually a 50 to 100 percent immediate return on your investment.

4. Pay off all debt but your mortgage as soon as possible: Pay the minimum required on all; pay more on the smallest until it's paid; then, apply that payment toward the next smallest until it's paid; repeat until all debts are paid off.

5. Complete your emergency fund: Save three- to six-months' living expenses, less if you're a two-income household, more if you're not. That should cover bigger problems like a job loss or medical emergency.

6. Invest *at least* 15 percent of your income: Raise your retirement plan contribution at work or start an Individual Retirement Account or Roth IRA.

7. Save for your children's college: Take advantage of tax-favored investment accounts.

8. Pay off your house early: Get completely out of debt.

9. Max out your retirement savings: invest the maximum allowed by your company or by the government; do more on your own.

10. Gain freedom: Achieve the ability to do whatever you want to do.

$8,000 yearly and depositing it in their institutions at the 8-percent interest they were paying at the time.

"This is doable," I thought.

And that's how I learned the value of **frugality, setting goals** and where necessary, **breaking them down into smaller subgoals** that could more easily be accomplished.

These realizations had a profound effect on my life, helping me to become wealthy.

But I'm not the first person to have these epiphanies.

First-generation rich

Dr. Thomas J. Stanley, America's foremost authority on the affluent and author of several award-winning books, surveyed millionaires for 20 years prior to writing *The Millionaire Next Door* in 1996. He discovered that 80 percent of America's millionaires were like me—first-generation rich.

How do you become wealthy? According to Stanley:

"It is seldom luck or inheritance or advanced degrees or even intelligence that enables people to amass fortunes. Wealth is more often the result of a lifestyle of hard work, perseverance, planning, and, most of all, self-discipline."[1]

Further, Stanley noted the millionaires he surveyed had similar lifestyles. Among their common characteristics, which I share, are:

1. **They live well beneath their means.**
2. **They allocate their time, energy and money efficiently, in ways conducive to building wealth.**
3. **They believe that financial independence is more important than displaying high social status.**
4. **Their parents did not provide economic outpatient care.**[2]

The latter point means that like me, they didn't get much financial help from their parents while they were alive or a great inheritance. These millionaires made their fortunes on their own.

What is "wealthy"?

Stanley decided to study the 95 percent of millionaires who had between $1 million and $10 million "because this level of wealth can be obtained in one generation. It can be obtained by many Americans".[3]

He added that he discovered that many people with high incomes —like doctors, lawyers and highly paid athletes—weren't wealthy; they were just living high on the hog.

So what is "wealthy"? Are you or am I "wealthy"?

Stanley reasoned that the more income you have, the wealthier you should be. Similarly, the longer you've been working, the more wealth you should have.

Based upon one's age and income, Stanley expected a certain level of wealth; he called people who have accumulated about what's expected Average Accumulators of Wealth. Those who spend more and have less than expected were Under Accumulators of Wealth.

To be truly wealthy, Stanley said you should have *twice* what you'd be expected to have, based on your age and income. He called these people 'Prodigious Accumulators of Wealth'.

To determine whether or not we are wealthy, no matter what your age or income level, he offered the following formula:

"Multiply your age times your realized pretax annual household income from all sources except inheritances. Divide by ten. This, less any inherited wealth, is what your net worth should be."[4]

Applying that to my last full year of work, 2011 (I retired upon turning 62 in October 2012), I calculated that my realized annual income from all sources was about $34,500. Multiplying it by 61 equals $2,104,500. Dividing it by 10 results in $210,450. Subtracting a $30,000 inheritance, which I received in 1998, my expected net worth, according to Stanley, should then have been $180,460. But my actual net worth at the end of 2011 was right at $500,000, a bit more than 2.75 times my expected net worth.

That made me a Prodigious Accumulator of Wealth, according to Stanley's definition.

As the old adage goes, **it's not what you make but what you save that counts.**

April and Ben

Another reason building wealth takes time, but can be done in one generation, is the miracle of **compound interest.**

When one invests an amount, interest is earned each year on the original amount and also on the interest earned in previous years. This accumulating interest compounds into a large amount over time as detailed below.

As you'll see in the following story of two young people I'll call April and Ben, it pays to start saving early because growing wealthy through compound interest takes time but pays off handsomely.

April started working at age 19 after graduating high school, diligently saving $2,000 a year for eight years. Then she got married and, as often happens, she became a mother. She decided to stay home to raise her children and run the household. She later returned to work but with her family responsibilities, she didn't add to the $16,000 she'd saved in those early years.

Fortunately, she left it in an investment account that gained 12 percent per year, which has been an often-quoted statistic of what the stock market has averaged historically.

Ben, on the other hand, got a good job after high school but he decided to have fun and didn't start saving like April did.

Eight years later though, he too fell in love, got married and started feeling the responsibilities of providing for a family and saving for retirement.

He started saving and investing $2,000 yearly for the rest of his working life, also earning 12 percent annually.

After 40 years, an amazing thing happened.

Due to compound interest, April's $16,000 grew to $1,035,425 — without her investing any more money.

Ben, by starting just eight years later, had only $682,851 — even though he invested $2,000 every year afterward, $64,000 by then. The accompanying table and the corresponding graph show how their investments grew yearly.

Compounding grows wealth

At 19, April invests $2,000 for eight years, then stops. Ben starts at 27, investing $2,000 yearly through age 65. Their investments grow 12 percent each year.

Age	April		Ben	
19	$2,000	$2,240	0	0
20	$2,000	$4,749	0	0
21	$2,000	$7,558	0	0
22	$2,000	$10,706	0	0
23	$2,000	$14,230	0	0
24	$2,000	$18,178	0	0
25	$2,000	$22,599	0	0
26	$2,000	$27,551	0	0
27	0	$30,857	$2,000	$2,240
28	0	$34,560	$2,000	$4,749
29	0	$38,708	$2,000	$7,558
30	0	$43,352	$2,000	$10,706
31	0	$48,554	$2,000	$14,230
32	0	$54,381	$2,000	$18,178
33	0	$60,907	$2,000	$22,599
34	0	$68,218	$2,000	$27,551
35	0	$76,802	$2,000	$33,097
36	0	$85,570	$2,000	$39,309
37	0	$95,383	$2,000	$46,266
38	0	$107,339	$2,000	$54,058
39	0	$120,220	$2,000	$62,785
40	0	$134,646	$2,000	$72,559
41	0	$150,804	$2,000	$83,506
42	0	$168,900	$2,000	$95,767
43	0	$189,168	$2,000	$109,499
44	0	$211,869	$2,000	$124,879
45	0	$237,293	$2,000	$142,104
46	0	$265,768	$2,000	$161,396
47	0	$297,660	$2,000	$183,004
48	0	$333,379	$2,000	$207,204
49	0	$373,385	$2,000	$234,308
50	0	$418,191	$2,000	$264,665
51	0	$468,374	$2,000	$298,665
52	0	$524,597	$2,000	$336,745
53	0	$587,528	$2,000	$379,394
54	0	$658,032	$2,000	$427,161
55	0	$736,995	$2,000	$480,660
56	0	$825,435	$2,000	$540,579
57	0	$924,487	$2,000	$607,688
58	0	$1,035,425	$2,000	$682,851
59	0	$1,159,676	$2,000	$767,033
60	0	$1,298,837	$2,000	$861,317
61	0	$1,454,698	$2,000	$966,915
62	0	$1,629,261	$2,000	$1,085,185
63	0	$1,824,773	$2,000	$1,217,647
64	0	$2,043,746	$2,000	$1,366,005
65	**0**	**$2,288,996**	**$2,000**	**$1,532,166**

Start saving as much as you can ASAP

The primary moral of this story is to **start saving as soon as you can**.

That may discourage someone who reads this later in life. But this is not the end of the story.

Even though Ben's investments never caught up to April's, his increased contributions did make a difference, especially when you compare what they had earned 10, 20 and 35 years from when they started. Ten years after she began saving and investing, April had $34,560; 10 years after he started, Ben had $39,309. After 20 years, April had $107,339; Ben had $161,396. And after 35 years, April had $658,032, while Ben had $966,915.

The second moral of this story is to **save as much as you can for as long as you can.**

According to the table, by the time they both reached age 65, April had $2,288,996, while Ben had $1,532,166.

You can't beat starting to save and invest early, but even with a late start, saving over a long time helped Ben achieve a comparable net worth.

I first encountered this example when our Iowa newspaper group established its first 401(k) retirement plan. But the two columns of numbers were just that. It was hard to see how this worked, and hard to understand the implications of the example, until I saw a graph of the numbers.

That made an impression on me, and I hope it will on you too.

The graph shows how April's and Ben's investments grew over 46 years at 12 percent interest. Over the first 20 years, notice that curve doesn't rise much; it only starts up in earnest after about 20–25 years, but after 30 years, it explodes.

That means you need to be patient. This is going to take a while.

What not to do

What you can't do if you hope to grow financially secure is get involved with addictive behaviors like excessive smoking or drinking, drugs, gambling or going into debt, other than for a 15-year mortgage. **If you're now in debt, you need to pay it off as soon as possible!**

Aside from the moral and health dimensions of such behaviors, or taking on debt, they're just too expensive! There's no way you can save for your future if you're overspending on addictive behaviors or paying for things twice by using debt.

As to the latter, a quote attributed to Dr. Albert Einstein on compound interest says it best:

"Compound interest is the eighth wonder of the world. He who understands it, earns it … he who doesn't … pays it."[5]

It works in real life

Lest you think this is not realistic, I overheard a friend, Barbara, telling another friend that she had seen $16,000, which was put into her 401(k) at work 25 years earlier, grow to $250,000. When I told her I wanted to use her story as an example, she added that she had done nothing; her employer had contributed the $16,000 for her and had decided how to invest it.

Compound interest not only works on paper but in the real world.

However, a student in one of Dave Ramsey's Financial Peace University classes that I've coordinated pooh-poohed the idea, saying he didn't want to scrimp and save for years, only to be too old to enjoy it by the time he accumulated it.

He missed the point. As you accumulate wealth, you can skim off a little for yourself; as you accumulate more, you can skim off a little more.

Real millionaires aren't like the ones portrayed on TV or in the movies. They don't live in mansions, drive exotic cars or wear designer clothes.

As Stanley notes in *The Millionaire Next Door*, real millionaires live in older middle-class to working-class neighborhoods. They drive late-model cars that aren't necessarily new and they wear the same department store clothes that most of us do.

What motivates them isn't materialism but financial security and the freedom to do whatever they want to do because they have the wherewithal to do so.

If that's what you'd like in your life, read on. This book is for you.

Compounding grows April's, Ben's savings handsomely

Growing at 12 percent annually, April's $16,000 that she saved from age 19 to 26, became $2,288,996 by age 65. By starting eight years later at age 27, Ben's $2,000 saved per year for 38 years grew to $1,532,166 by age 65.

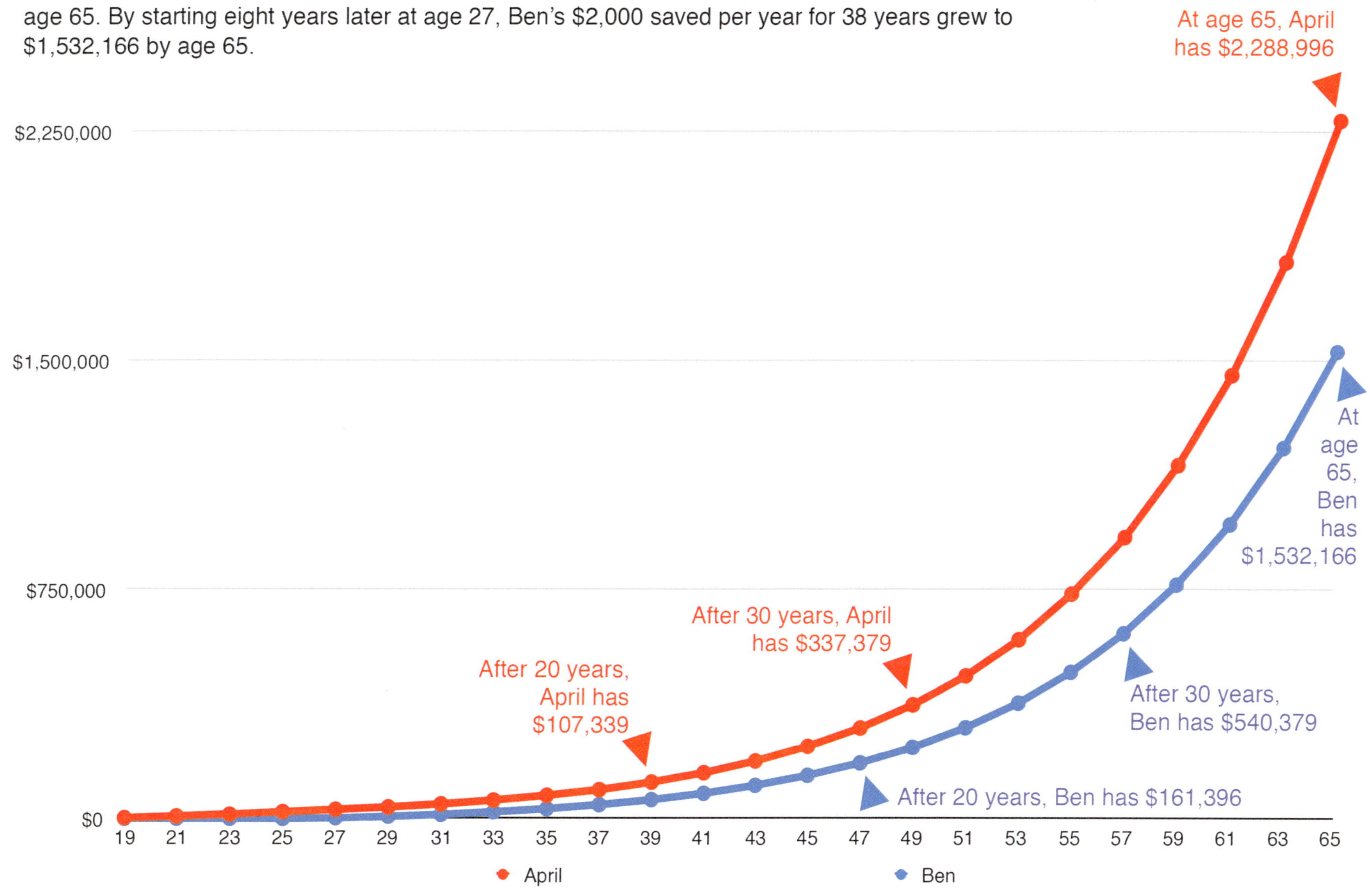

A pair of boaters cross Diamond Lake, Michigan, just after sunset on a summer evening.

"The man is the richest whose pleasures are the cheapest."

— HENRY DAVID THOREAU

CHAPTER 2

Learn to live well, beneath your means

Frugality is the key to millionaires' success

I'm a bit of a clotheshorse, another trait I gained from my mother.

Several times when I coordinated Financial Peace University classes at church, on the evening of the lesson on how to get great deals, I wore a Christian Dior, Arrow or Eddie Bauer shirt, dress slacks by Austin Reed of London, a Dockers argyle sweater, a NAUTICA jacket and black Johnston & Murphy handcrafted tassel loafers.

I told my students that all but the sweater came from one of my favorite clothiers—Goodwill.

Several years ago, as I was planning to coordinate this class, I found the sweater and thought it matched the outfit very well. It was on a Sears clearance table for $8.

As noted in the first chapter, Dr. Thomas J. Stanley wrote in *The Millionaire Next Door* that one of the traits of America's real millionaires is that **they live well beneath their means.**[1]

I prefer to **live well, beneath my means.**

These are examples of how to do that.

A woman advertising salesperson, who always had to look good for her job, told me that she and her daughter also periodically take a Saturday and peruse thrift shops.

"Why buy jeans anywhere else?" she asked.

Why indeed? I've never understood why one would pay good money on pre-washed jeans—or worse, acid washed jeans or those with holes in them that are supposed to look worn but just look phony.

You can find better-looking jeans in a thrift store for just a few dollars.

My advertising salesperson friend also noted thrift stores are where she shopped for her husband's sport coats, and I do too.

Ditto for dress pants, shirts and khakis.

I always make sure they fit well, and I look them over closely for stains or wear. But I've been able to find gently used clothing that fit well and look great.

At the point in my life, I don't need to buy clothes at Goodwill, but my attitude is, "Why should I spend more than I need to."

Shopping thrift stores is a habit I also picked up from my mother. In her later years, she volunteered in a local thrift store and frequented them to buy gifts of clothing for her grandchildren. I sometimes thought my siblings and their spouses looked askance at these gifts, because shopping in secondhand stores wasn't fashionable then. But she didn't care, and I acquired her frugal ways.

Thrifting now fashionable

Now, even fashion-conscious teens talk about their thrift-store finds.

In a July 30, 2013, *Knoxville News Sentinel* article, "Back-to-school Thrifting," rising senior Natalie Porter reported that her biggest coup was finding a Louis Vuitton handbag, in near-mint condition, which she estimated was worth close to $200, for $10.

She added she's also scored a North Face jacket on Goodwill's half-price day for $10 and a New York & Co. dress that she wore to Cotillion and Winter Formal for $15.[2]

Similarly, I now have among the lesser treasures in my closet, a pair of brand-new Dockers khakis with the tags still attached that I bought for $15, the NAUTICA jacket I bought for $8, and perhaps my best find, the aforementoned Johnston&Murphy handcrafted tassel loafers, valued on the company's website at $175, that I bought on a Goodwill half-price day for $1.50.

Thrift stores are also a good place to look for small appliances and electronics. Usually, these items are so inexpensively priced that even if they wear out in a year or two, you're still money ahead over paying retail for new ones. Such items I've bought in thrift stores have lasted for years.

The article also noted more young people are shopping thrift stores because **they believe in reusing and recycling; they don't look at thrift-store clothing as hand-me-downs.**[3]

Being good stewards

That's nothing new to me. I was brought up in the 1950s and 1960s, where I was taught to be a good steward, to make the most of and not squander God's gifts.

I was brought up to always turn off the light when leaving a room so as not to waste electricity. I made many of my toys out of scrap wood and cardboard. And I gained my spending money as a preteen by scrounging soda pop bottles to return for the nickel deposits.

My mother was born into an era where flour sacks were made of fabric that could be re-used to make clothes, and of course, hand-me-downs were a way of life.

And she sewed throughout her life, even parlaying her knowledge of sewing and fabrics into a salesclerk's job in a dry goods store.

In addition to sewing many of her own clothes, she sewed me a sport coat and my sister Linda's wedding dress. In later years, she saved scraps of material and sewed quilts to give to all of her children and grandchildren and to donate to church sales.

My older sister, Velma, recalled mom being able to "make something from nothing".

My parents both grew up on farms and kept a garden in the backyard of their home; they bought eggs from a local farmer, and they would buy a quarter of beef from a meat locker, the various cuts of which they kept in a chest-type deep freeze in the basement.

Occasionally my father would get a pheasant from a local hunter, which he would clean.

I also remember once as a small child seeing a small cage containing several live chickens in the garage, which I presumed would be butchered.

Attitude adjustment needed

As noted above, in high school, I learned we were socio-economically "working poor," although **I never felt poor**. And not only the working poor lived this way.

I once interviewed an engineer friend, Richard Pugh, who'd grown up during the Great Depression. This was an assignment for a college-level American history term paper.

He was the son of a lawyer, whose family kept a garden and raised chickens in the backyard, which was common in their town during the 1920s. He noted they even spliced together broken leather shoestrings, shaving off the ends of the leather pieces so they could be sewn back together at the same thickness as the original.

I'm not suggesting we go back to sewing our own clothes, raising chickens or splicing together shoestrings. I'm just pointing out that **our forefathers had a mindset of using—and reusing—what was available to them** that we've largely lost in twenty-first-century America. Trying to recover that mindset would go a long way toward making us financially secure.

My mother told us a story from the 1930s where my father stooped to pick a penny off the sidewalk only to be told by another man, "I wouldn't bend my back for a penny". That man, apparently too lazy to pick up a penny at a time when it actually could buy something, never did amount to much, according to my mother.

I still pick up pennies—they help pay sales tax—and also paper clips and rubber bands. I reuse envelopes that come with bills that I'm paying through direct debit, to pay other bills; I reuse dry-cleaning bags for taking out garbage, and I run paper that's clean on one side through my ink-jet printer for projects that won't leave home.

Admittedly, I may take this to extreme. But I also never have to buy rubber bands or paper clips. As Dave Ramsey, personal finance expert, bestselling author and host of the Dave Ramsey Show, has said:

"Normal is broke; I don't want to be normal".[4]

Other ideas

Some other money-saving ideas that I practice:

• Borrowing books and DVDs from the public library rather than buying them or subscribing to cable TV or a streaming service. My local library has a good selection of recent releases, and if all the copies of a particular movie are checked out, I can reserve a copy.

If I'm looking for something to watch over the weekend, I'll go to the library in midweek. If I need to reserve something, chances are good that a copy will have come back by the time I want to watch it.

• Looking for books, CDs and DVDs that I want to keep at quarterly or yearly library book sales. For those that I don't find there, Knoxville, Tenn., near where I live, also has a great used-book store.

• Only watching broadcast TV. I know from previously having cable that it is just too expensive for what benefit I get from it. I can get over 30 channels with a high-definition antenna.

A student in one of my classes also pondered cutting the cable and realized that doing so would give him more time to read a stack of books he'd accumulated.

I do like some of the new drama series that have been offered on cable TV channels or streaming. But I've found them—and some of my favorite shows and movies from yesteryears—rerun on broadcast TV's new digital channels. Or I've found DVD sets of recent TV series at the public library. In the latter case, I can borrow a DVD set for three weeks. When there's nothing on TV that I want to watch, I pop in a DVD and watch an episode from one of those series.

• Buying cell phones and services that don't require contracts. I bought my first two cell phones from Tracfone. I kept one as a backup, for which I paid $200 for three years' service, after I decided to buy a smartphone. That was an iPhone I bought through Sprint, now T-Mobile, for $68 per month, including a hotspot for an Internet connection, which I use both at home and away. And the hotspot is sufficient for watching video though probably not for streaming.

Clothes, cable TV and cell phones are three areas where you can spend a lot of money in short order; hence the examples above. But there are many ways in which you can save a few dollars every day—which add up—while only minimally affecting your lifestyle.

A few more suggestions:

• Microwave a breakfast sandwich and brew coffee at home, and take a travel mug with you rather than stopping at McDonald's or Starbuck's (Some call it Five Bucks) en route to work.

• Choose water as a default drink of choice when dining out rather than a soft drink or coffee. I used to automatically choose a soft drink, especially at a fast-food restaurant. Now, if I'm in the mood for one, I'll have one, but most often I'm just as happy with water. It saves a bit and is healthier.

• Use coupons but only for items you would buy anyway or that you're positive you'll use. Two grocery stores where I shop also have gas pumps and offer discounts with every $100 or $150 in groceries purchased in a month's time.

Key to building wealth

Dr. Stanley noted that frugality was the key to building wealth for the millionaires he surveyed. **They make frugality—the efficient use of resources—a way of life.**[5]

"How did the wife of a millionaire respond when her husband gave her $8 million worth of stock in the company he recently took public? According to her husband of thirty-one years, she said, 'I appreciate this, I really do'. Then she smiled, never changing her position at the kitchen table, where she continued to cut twenty-five- and fifty-cents off food coupons from the week's supply of newspapers. … She just does today like she has always done, even when all we owned was a kitchen table. … It's how come we're well-off today. …"[6]

And this doesn't have to cramp your lifestyle. If you really need your Starbucks in the morning, OK. If you're a sports junkie, and you really want cable TV to keep up with your teams, so be it; just buy the package you need and economize elsewhere.

We all have our favorite activities that aren't economical but we can make up for them in other ways.

This isn't meant to turn you into a penny-pinching hoarder; it's intended to help get rid of bad habits and make you **more purposeful in your spending**. And to give you more money to save for what's truly important to you, which we'll discuss further. First, you need to save for an emergency fund, which is the subject of the next chapter.

CHAPTER 3

Save first for an emergency

Stuff happens, and it can happen to you at any time

One day in May 2010, I was driving down Kingston Pike in Knoxville, Tenn. I was in the outside lane; I sensed someone drifting into my lane, and I veered to avoid him, striking the curb. I could feel that I had blown a tire.

Fortunately, I was able to pull into a driveway, getting out of the flow of traffic.

A passerby stopped and offered to help change the tire but a closer inspection showed that I had blown both passenger-side tires.

That meant I needed a tow. I wasn't then an AAA member but it was the only place I was referred to by directory assistance.

Cost: $64.

AAA towed me to a Firestone store. They told me that in addition to having two flat tires, I had bent a wheel rim.

They looked for a replacement wheel in Knoxville but couldn't find one. A new one would cost $200 and would take a week to arrive.

Since I lived a half-hour away from there, I bought a low-priced tire from Firestone to

Firefighters approach a natural gas fire from behind a shield of water.

put on the good wheel rim and used the small doughnut spare tire so I could get home and use my regular sources to make permanent repairs.

Cost: $140.32.

I had a friend who dealt in used cars; fortunately he had a replacement for my 2001 Ford Focus styled steel wheel.

That was fortunate because the wheel was rare; I was told Ford changed the wheel style and size the next year, and it was even a different size than the standard wheel for the 2001 Focus.

Cost: $75.

Having a replacement wheel, I went to the tire store I normally deal with to get a new tire.

Cost: $177.42.

Since I hit the curb hard enough to blow two tires and bend a wheel rim, I reasoned that I should have the front end realigned to prevent excessive wear to the new tires.

But upon putting my car up on the hoist, a tire-store employee informed me that I had a bent tie rod as well. That would have to be replaced before he could correctly align the front end.

This necessitated a trip to my favorite mechanic. He noted more front-end work needed to be done. He replaced both front struts, both inner and outer tie rods on the passenger side, the passenger-side sway bar link and brake pads and rotors.

Cost: $868.29.

A final trip to the tire store to have the alignment cost an additional $65.50.

Total cost to get my car back to where it needed to be: $1,390.53.

That—or something like it—will happen to you too. That's why your first savings goal should be to set up an emergency fund.

Start with $1,000, preferably more

Dave Ramsey's first step—which he advises doing as fast as possible—is saving $1,000 and putting it in the bank for emergencies, which will invariably happen.[1]

Murphy's Law: Anything that can go wrong will go wrong

There's nothing magical about $1,000; it's just a nice round figure that should cover most day-to-day emergencies, such as fixing a car breakdown that keeps you from getting to work.

But a $1,000 emergency fund wouldn't have been enough for me in the situation detailed above. With rising prices, you might want to start by saving $1,500 or $2,000.

But **start with something and raise it to three to six months of living expenses as soon as you can**. That should cover most typical emergencies such as broken limbs, minor surgeries, car repairs or tiding you over if you're laid off from work.

You may get by with three-months' expenses if your family has more than one income; if you're relying on one paycheck, you need to be able to cover six months' expenses.

At the time of the accident above, I had an emergency fund that would cover about six months' living expenses, so I was able to cover the car repairs. Although I grumbled every time I had to write another check, at least I had the money to pay cash all the way through.

Had I only had $1,000 in my emergency fund, it still would have helped a lot.

I might have gotten an estimate from my mechanic before doing the front-end work, or I might have been able to pay that bill in several installments.

The key point is that these type of emergencies can—and will—happen at any time to anyone, and saving $1,000 or more—quickly! —is a good first step toward meeting them.

But that is just a start. You need a fund that equals at least three-to six-months' living expenses to cover more costly emergencies, like a medical emergency or loss of a job.

'Murphy repellant'

Ramsey says that having an emergency fund is "Murphy repellant".[2]

In other words, Murphy's Law—anything that can go wrong, will—applies more to those who don't have emergency funds.

This sounds intuitively true but have you thought about why it's so?

One reason is that when we don't have much money, we'll opt for the cheapest solution to fix a problem, which may not be the best solution; therefore we may soon have further problems and higher repair bills.

Had I not thought to have my alignment checked, I might have worn out the two front tires fairly quickly and soon faced another big expense.

As it was, come November 2, 2010, I walked outside to find the "low-priced" tire I had bought from Firestone flat.

Since I was now an AAA member, I called them to come and fix it. The repairman found a nail in the tread but he also found a tear in the tire wall where it attached to the rim. That couldn't be fixed.

This required me to go back to my tire dealer for another tire, which cost me an additional $88.71.

Now, the total cost of replacing the wheel and tires reached $1,479.24.

I don't blame Firestone. I got what I asked for—a cheap tire. But going the cheap route invited Murphy back into my life.

No more living paycheck to paycheck

I once tried to relate the importance of saving $1,000 for emergencies to a pair of co-workers.

One immediately stifled the conversation. "I could never do that," she said, and that was the end of the discussion.

That's a self-fulfilling prophesy: **If you're convinced that you can't do something, you won't be able to.**

And should she have an emergency, I assume she'd do what a lot of people would do: put the emergency expense on a credit card at 16 to 20 percent interest.[3]

But if she's already living paycheck to paycheck—as she apparently was—where would she find the money to pay back the credit card plus the interest that would accrue for however long it would take her to pay off the debt?

This is how many people get deeply into credit card debt—using a credit card for "emergencies" but not having a plan to pay off the additional debt they just incurred plus the interest that the credit card company will charge them.

If you can't pay off any debt put on a credit card within 30 days, cut it up; you can't afford it.

The other co-worker was a bit more open-minded, saying she could do without cable TV if she had to.

She has since gone on to a better-paying job. I hope she has used those extra resources to put herself on a path to financial prosperity.

If you're now living paycheck to paycheck like the first co-worker in the example above, you need to ask yourself what you can do to start on a path to prosperity.

You may need to try to work some overtime, get a second job for a while, or—like the second co-worker—be willing to sacrifice something for a while.

I believe most people can find ways to live more frugally, which is why I made living well, beneath my means, my first step on the journey to prosperity.

Even if you get a better job like the second employee in the example above, you will still have to learn frugality if you want to build an emergency fund, pay off your debts, save for a house, cars and the other luxuries of life, help children pay for college and have a comfortable retirement.

Otherwise, it's too easy to just spend more as your income improves; then you're still in the same boat, living paycheck to paycheck.

And although it's necessary to save money to gain the finer material things in life, living frugally doesn't have to be a drag, as was shown in the last chapter.

Next, you need to create a bucket list of what you *really* want.

If you're convinced that you can't do something, you won't be able to.

CHAPTER 4

Dreams can come true

Set goals and deadlines for what you want to do

Remember the movie, "The Bucket List," starring Morgan Freeman and Jack Nicholson.

Both characters, Nicholson's billionaire hospital magnate and Freeman's relatively poor auto mechanic, came to be hospital roommates after being told they were terminally ill and had about a year to live.

As they mused about their situation, they decided to compile a "bucket list," a wish list of things they wanted to do before they "kicked the bucket." Using Nicholson's vast resources and private jet — they set off to accomplish their list of goals.

First came skydiving, then racing classic cars around a speedway.

Next came a trip around the world, including flying over the North Pole, going on a lion safari in Africa, marveling at the Taj Mahal in India, riding motorcycles atop the Great Wall of China and dining on fine cuisine at Chevre d'Or in France.[1] The only thing they're unable to accomplish is taking in the view from Mount Everest because it is shrouded in clouds.

Create your own bucket list

Step 1: Make a list of everything that you'd like to have, see, be or do. Dream big; be as specific as you can. Imagine you have unlimited time, talent and resources. What would you do?

List as many items as you can. There's no time limit. Compile as many as you can in one sitting, then come back to it later.

Most importantly, don't try to analyze the items as to whether they're realistic; that will come later.

Step Two: Rank the items as to how important they are to you. Put a No. 1 beside anything you absolutely want to do before you die. Put a No. 2 beside anything you really want to do but don't feel that strongly about. Put a No. 3 beside items that you want to do but in which you wouldn't be terribly disappointed if they didn't happen.

Step Three: Set up separate sheets of paper with headings for different categories of goals: social, spiritual, mental, physical, family, financial, career, relationship, status and any other categories that make sense to you.

On each sheet, make subcategories based on how soon you hope to accomplish a goal. Set deadlines like "To do as soon as possible," "To do within one year," "To do within two to five years," "To do within 10 years," "To do within my lifetime". Set time frames that make sense to you.

Using the suggested deadlines above, your financial goals sheet might look like the following:

FINANCIAL GOALS
To do within one year:
Save $2,000 for emergencies.
Set up a monthly budget.
To do within 2–5 years:
Pay off all debt except home mortgage.
Build an emergency fund of six-months expenses.
Start saving 15 percent of income into a 401(k) and a Roth IRA.
To do within 6–10 years:
Accelerate payments to pay off 15-year mortgage early.
Have $_________ set aside for children's college education. (Set a specific amount, even if it's a guess. It will give you a specific goal to work toward).
To do by retirement at age 62–67:
Have $_________ in retirement savings.
Give $_________ annually to your church and other charities.

A small float plane prepares to take off along the Chena River near Fairbanks, Alaska.

"Keep away from people who try to belittle your ambitions. Small people always do that, but the really great make you feel that you too can become great."

— MARK TWAIN

After these adventures, the men realize that family is most important. Freeman's character returns for his last dinner with his wife, children and grandchildren, and Nicholson's character reconciles with his estranged daughter, crossing off his "kiss the most beautiful girl in the world" goal upon meeting his granddaughter and giving her a peck on the cheek.

One of the points the movie makes is that we often put off making our goals and seeking to accomplish them until we're at a point that it's now or never.

As noted in Chapter 3, **being frugal on the everyday, routine expenses of life isn't intended to make you a miser but rather to make more money available to spend on what's most important to you.**

That begs the next question: What's important to you? You may already have some things in mind but I maintain that everyone—even if you're 19 years old, in perfect health and can expect to live to be 95—needs a "bucket list."

Dave Ramsey advises that the time to start saving for a house down payment is after acquiring your three-to-sixth months' emergency fund.[2] This is also a good time to start a bucket list, which will probably include many of the goals he recommends.

Start with a 'dream list'

I first became acquainted with this idea while in my 20's, when I was a member of the U.S. Jaycees. A Jaycees' manual, *Personal Dynamics*, advised starting to set

Break a big goal down into manageable subgoals

Want to retire a millionaire by age 65. Depending upon your age and what you already have saved, you would have to save the following amounts monthly, and earn 8 percent yearly, to reach that overall goal.

If you are age:	and you have saved:	each month, you must save:
35	$200,000	**$0**
	$100,000	**$0**
	$50,000	**$304**
	$0	**$671**
45	$200,000	**$25**
	$100,000	**$861**
	$50,000	**$1,298**
	$0	**$1,698**
55	$200,000	**$3,040**
	$100,000	**$4,253**
	$50,000	**$4,859**
	$0	**$5,466**

Source: Kiplinger's Personal Finance

goals by first compiling a "dream list."

"Write down everything you have ever wanted to have, to see, to do, to be, etc. Don't prejudge! Write everything down. Add to the list continually. Get a minimum of 100 items. This exercise will give you insight into your wants."[3]

I was never able to think of at least 100 items, not even 50. I think I made it to about 35. But do as many as you can. There's no time limit either. Compile as many as you can at one sitting, then come back to it a day or two later. Just don't put it off indefinitely.

Also, don't try to analyze your "dream list" items as to whether they are realistic or not while making the list; that will come later. Your mind cannot think creatively and analytically at the same time. If you try to analyze your choices as you go along, you'll shut down your creative impulses.

So if you're a middle-age woman and have always wanted to be a ballerina or a princess, write it down; if you're a middle-age man who's dreamed of being a football star, write it down. Personally, I've always dreamed of being a secret agent. Don't eliminate seemingly impossible dreams.

The Jaycees' publication next called for spelling out goals in these six areas of one's life: **social, spiritual, mental, physical, family and financial**.[4] In my personal goal setting, I added several categories of my own, which I detail in the accompanying "Create your own bucket list" sidebar. Feel free to add your own categories and subtract any that don't make sense to you.

Establish priorities

Once you've completed the list, you can start evaluating the individual items.

I like to divide such lists into three parts, those things I feel most strongly about, those things that I want to do but don't feel as strongly about, and those things that I'd like to do but that I won't be disappointed about if I don't do them. This is a quick and easy way to begin prioritizing your "dream list."

I'm a firm believer that you can accomplish just about anything you set your mind to but you can't do everything. That's why, after listing everything, you need to prioritize them. You'll want to work hardest on your No. 1 choices, next hardest on the No. 2s, and pick up as many No. 3s as you can along the way.

Next, your **priorities need deadlines** by which they should be accomplished.

As described in the accompanying sidebar, put flexible deadlines by when you'd like to achieve your No. 1 priorities. Then, do the same for your No. 2 priorities. If you wish, you can do the same for your No. 3s.

Again, I like to keep it pretty simple because deadlines will change with changing circumstances. Choose a close deadline, six months or a year, for those goals you can accomplish right away. Choose an intermediate deadline, like three to five years, for those that will take a bit more time to accomplish, And choose one or two longer deadlines, like 10 years or "by retirement," for your longer-term goals.

Many other goal-setting exercises encourage you to break goals down into smaller steps that will lead you to your goals. That's the best way to ensure that you'll reach your goals, but it's also a lot of work. I've also read that just writing down a specific goal and a reasonable deadline will substantially improve your chances of achieving it over just thinking about what you want. So write them down and be specific. Write "I want to have $1 million by age 65," not just "I want to retire wealthy."

Some goals, like buying a newer used car within 2-5 years, won't require a lot more planning than just saving up the money. Others, like losing 20 pounds within a year, will require further planning steps: checking with your doctor as to your current health, setting a subgoal to lose 2 pounds per month for example, choosing appropriate daily exercise and deciding what you can eat on a daily basis.

You'll have to choose which goals need to be divided into subgoals, then make an action plan for achieving them.

I first realized that having $1 million by age 65 was a realistic goal after seeing the Federal Reserve's prime interest rate shoot up to 20 percent in 1980.[5] Banks' TV advertisements then noted that you could make $1 million by saving $8,000 per year and investing it at 8 percent over 40 years.

That is a classic example of breaking a big goal into smaller, manageable pieces.

And for those seemingly impossible dreams, think about what it is you most like about being a ballerina, princess or football star. If you'd like to dance gracefully, you can take classes to do that; if you like dressing in fancy clothes and attending balls like a princess, you can find a way to do that. Or you can express your love of football by coaching kids or refereeing. I know of a retired hospital administrator who for years expressed his love of the game by refereeing Division I college football.

What if life gets in the way?

"How can I plan for the rest of my life?" you may be thinking as you ponder creating a bucket list. "I could change my mind—by tomorrow. Or more likely, something will get in the way so I won't achieve my goal."

Will things change before you get to achieve your written goals? Of course they will!

The point of this exercise is not to set things in stone but to urge you to **think about what you want in life and set some reasonable expectations** about when you might be able to achieve them.

I advise couples to each make their own lists, then compare notes because you'll have to make accommodations with each other as to when you can finance each other's goals, especially the bigger ones.

File your lists and bring them back out once a year or so and consider if you still want to achieve them.

Things will change as you go along; some No. 1's will no longer be important and will move down in priority to No. 2 or No. 3, or move off the list entirely, while something else that wasn't even on your original list will jump onto it as a No. 1 priority.

Also, as you review your lists yearly, you'll come across items that you said several years ago that you wanted to accomplish by now. Then you'll need to ask yourself, "Do I still want to do this now?" If yes, you'd better get cracking and figure out how you're going to get it done. If not now, you can either move it further down on the timeline or drop it all together.

Compiling a "bucket list" and reviewing your goals every year or two will **keep them at the top of your mind.**

As noted in an earlier chapter, one student in a class I coordinated pooh-poohed the call to live cheaply and save as much as possible for retirement, saying he didn't want to end up rich at age 80, then not be able to

A downed tree branch lies along Chilhowee Lake in East Tennessee.

"A life that hasn't a definite plan is likely to become driftwood."

— DAVID SARNOFF

enjoy it. He missed the point. As you attain more, you can skim a little off. As you attain more and more, you can skim more off. And a "bucket list" gives you ideas for skimming.

Too many people drift through life. You'll hear them saying regretfully, "I wish I would have done this." Or, "If I'd had the money, I would have done that."

If you complete this simple exercise and review it every year or two, you certainly won't achieve every goal on your list; you may not achieve most of them.

But if you're like me, by keeping this list on the top of your mind, you probably will achieve most of your life goals that are most important to you. And by then, many of the other items on the list won't matter any more.

To keep your plans on track is the subject of Chapter 6: budgeting.

A sculpture at the Franklin Delano Roosevelt Memorial in Washington, D. C., depicts a Great Depression scene.

"Debt is the worst poverty."

— THOMAS FULLER

CHAPTER 5

Avoid debt except for a home mortgage

Pay off your existing debt as soon as you possibly can

My mother, as a survivor of the Great Depression, always counseled that those who had cash came out of the depression OK.

As I pondered what she meant, I decided that she was saying that those who survived best were those who avoided going into debt. If they had cash to take care of themselves, and they didn't owe anything to anyone else, they would be OK.

My mother and father never went into debt, except for buying a house. They didn't buy anything until and unless they could pay cash for it.

Delaying gratification of my wants was an important lesson I learned from my parents—one that has been key to my financial success. But that is a lesson that I fear has been lost on many if not most Americans today.

Debt is not your friend

Debt has made it too easy to buy things we want as opposed to things we need, and unfortunately, I fear it has led to too many people spending too much on junk and not on the high-quality items that they'd want in the long run.

Should I buy this?

Ask yourself these questions before buying anything.
1. **Do I *really* want this?** (Avoid impulse purchases by waiting overnight or at least an hour or two)
2. **Can I pay cash for this?** (If the answer is no, you can't afford it.)
3. **Will buying this mean that I won't have enough money for something else that I need or want more?** (If the answer is yes, you can't afford it.)

Many people have gotten into credit card debt not by buying something they really wanted but by not having a plan for their day-to-day spending, so when the unexpected occurred—like home or car repairs—they used the credit card to make up for their lack of planning and disciplined saving.[1]

Or maybe people fall deeply into debt simply because they can; it is easy to do.

After moving to Tennessee, I refinanced my house twice as interest rates fell. At one

---

of the loan closings, my lender told the lawyer who was handling the closing about a married couple who had taken out a home equity loan and couldn't pay it back.

"Where'd all this money go?" asked the lender.

The wife replied that they'd grown up in the Great Depression and never had anything, so now that they had some money, they were going to spend it—apparently on miscellaneous purchases that couldn't be returned or sold for much.

Even worse, the lawyer noted, was that the home equity loan they'd taken out wouldn't be forgiven if they filed for bankruptcy. If they couldn't pay the loan back, they could lose their house.

The moral of this story is to learn to delay gratification of your wants until you can pay cash for them.

Plan for your lesser wants as you prepare your monthly budget, and put larger wants on the bucket list I gave you in the last chapter.

Debt Snowball

If you are in debt and can at least make the minimum monthly payments on all your debts, you may find the Debt Snowball method, detailed in an accompanying box, an effective way to get all your debts paid off as quickly as possible. Essentially, you list your debts from smallest to largest and, while continuing to make all minimum payments, put extra money toward paying off the smallest debt first. Once it's paid, you apply what you had paid toward it to the next smallest debt, and so on, until you've paid them all off.

Mathematically, it would be best to pay off higher interest debt first. But paying off small debts first gives you quick psychological victories and encourages you to keep going as you attack the bigger ones.

For example, if you had $2,000 of debt, which you were able to acquire at 5 percent interest, and you had $10,000 in debt at 18 percent interest, knocking out the smaller one quickly would give you a sense of accomplishment, which would hopefully give you the energy to attack the big one.

However, if the two were similar in size, say $8,000 in 5-percent debt and $9,000 in 18-percent debt, I'd consider attacking the 18-percent debt first. They're both going to take a while to pay off—there'll be no quick victory—so you'd be better off getting rid of the higher-interest debt first.

Loans from family

Except when I purchased part ownership in the weekly newspaper chain my partners and I owned in Iowa, and when I bought two houses, which I'll talk about in another chapter, I think the only time I went into debt was to borrow a few hundred dollars from my mother to buy my first or second needed car—I subsequently paid her back over a couple months.

And when I borrowed the money to purchase the part interest in the newspaper firm, I entered into a business deal with my mother; we could make a more mutually beneficial deal than either of us could do on our own. I paid her 7 3/4 percent interest, which was more than what she could get on a certificate of deposit, and it was less than what I would have to pay on a bank loan.

It's generally unwise to borrow from family members or loan money to them. The borrower will promise to pay back the loan, but many times they won't, which will put strain on the family relationship. This relationship is more important than any loan!

Snowball pays off debts quickly

The following procedure, known as the Debt Snowball, is a good way to pay off a number of debts quickly.

List all debts from smallest to largest with the smallest balance first.

Make the minimum payment on every debt, and add whatever you can per month to pay off the smallest debt as soon as possible.

Then, add that debt's monthly payment to the minimum payment on the second smallest debt to repay it as quickly as possible.

Repeat until all debts are paid in full.

By the time larger debts are reached, the extra amount paid toward them will grow quickly, similar to a snowball rolling downhill gathering more snow (hence the name).

An example of the Debt Snowball in action is shown below. This person has an additional $100 per month, which can be devoted to repayment of debt.

Creditor	Balance	Minimum Payment	New Payment	Payments Remaining	Cumulative Payments
Visa	$250	$25/mo.	$125/mo.	2	2
Balance paid in 2 months					
MasterCard	$500	$26/mo.	$151/mo.	3	5
Balance $448 after 2 months, paid in another 3 months					
Car Payment	$2,500	$150/mo.	$301/mo.	6	11
Balance $1,750 after 5 months, paid in another 6 months					
Loan	$5,000	$200/mo.	$501/mo.	6	17
Balance $2,800 after 11 months, paid in another 6 months					

Thus, in 17 months, this person has repaid four debts, with two of them being paid in a mere five months and three within one year.

In our case, my mother and I—being like-minded—treated it as a business relationship. I obtained a promissory note form from my local banker, which I filled out and gave to my mother. My banker also printed an amortization schedule detailing how much of each month's payment was for principal reduction and interest.

I followed that repayment schedule until she died, then paid each of my siblings their share of what was still due. This is the only way I would handle a loan between family members.

You don't need to borrow to establish credit

One thing my mother stressed to me as a young adult was that one didn't need to borrow, such as on a credit card, to establish a good credit rating.

She maintained that one could do so by being responsible and paying bills on time.

That was contrary to conventional wisdom. I even interviewed a small-town banker during the late 1970s who had advised his daughter to use a credit card to build up her credit score.

My experiences have shown me that my mother was right. Even Fair Isaac Corporation (FICO), which reports credit scores, notes that 35 percent of your credit score—the biggest chunk—is determined by your payment history.

Another 30 percent is determined by the ratio of what you owe to the amount of credit that's available to you; the less you owe, the better.[2] Owing nothing is best.

I honestly never knew my credit score when I sought to finance the two homes I purchased. And I never had a problem getting a mortgage.

Only in checking old records dating to 2002 when I last refinanced the loan on my current home—research for writing this chapter—did I discover that my FICO credit score was then 717, just 23 points shy of what was considered "very good".[3]

A banker friend said **there are two things you need to take out a loan: the capacity to repay it and good character**, measured objectively by your credit score.

Having a good credit score is helpful, because most automatic underwriting is done by a computer algorithm. However, if you have a unique financial situation, manual underwriting—a human being looks at your finances like my mother would—can improve your chances of getting a loan, according to Rocket Mortgage®.

A lender might manually underwrite a loan if you live debt-free and have no credit score, like Dave Ramsey; if you're self-employed; if you're young or new to the country and haven't yet built up a credit score; if you've had past financial problems or if you have a debt-to-income (DTI) ratio that's too high.

The lender will ask for quite a bit of documentation: verification of other assets you own, like vehicles or homes; recent pay stubs to show consistent, reliable income and your credit report to ensure that your payment history is consistent and on-time. The lender may contact your employer about bonuses or commissions and your work history, to judge the chances of your leaving in the near future.

Your underwriter will look at your financial obligations to see how much of your income goes toward expenses like credit card payments, rent, loan payments, child support, back taxes or other court-ordered judgments. He wants to know that you'll be able to afford the mortgage in addition to other debts.

Finally, the lender will look at the collateral for the loan, the value of the property and size of the downpayment.[4]

A high FICO score can make getting a mortgage easier—but the trade-off isn't worth it if car loans and credit card payments limit your ability to save.

Reasons for a credit card

I had and used credit cards in the days before debit cards became available.

My first was a Standard Oil credit card provided by my employer to pay for expenses when I was on the road.

The main thing I learned was that I could submit an expense report and get paid immediately after returning from a trip, yet have 30 to 60 days before I was billed for the credit card charges. That gave me Standard Oil's money to use during that time.

I put it in my checking-with-interest account until I needed to pay the bill (always on time). It was only worth a few bucks but they stayed in my pocket. An entrepreneur was born.

Since then, I've owned several credit cards, mainly using them to buy gas, again always paying them off on time.

Once I was able to get a debit card from my bank, I did so and never looked back. I've used debit cards for everything for which I used to use a credit card. Despite being told about not being able to use a debit card in some situations, I've never had any problem using one to reserve a hotel room, rent a car or buy anything online.

Even though you don't need to borrow to build credit, my banker friend gave me several good reasons for having and using a credit card occasionally—**always paying the balance immediately when it comes due.**

The first is that when one uses a debit card to reserve a room or rent a car, the seller will put a hold on your bank account in the amount of the room or car rental. So, if you don't otherwise have enough in your checking account for other purchases, you might run short. And if you don't have enough in the account when you're trying to reserve the room or car, you may be denied —even though you will have money in the account by the time you will pay for the room or the car rental.

With a credit card, the room or car rental hold comes off your line of credit, not the money in your bank account.

Secondly, in the case of identity theft, using a credit card puts your line of credit at risk, not the money in your bank account.

My bank's customer service representative assured me that if money is stolen through fraudulent use of a debit card, you'll most likely get a provisional credit for the money taken while the bank investigates to make sure the money was stolen. That takes 30 to 45 days to determine.

Shackles are shown at Brushy Mountain State Penitentiary in Petros, Tennessee.

"The rich rule over the poor, and the borrower is a slave to the lender."

— PROVERBS 22: 7

She noted it also might take the credit card issuer 30 to 45 days to determine that the charges made weren't yours. But then, only your credit is dinged, not the money in your bank account.

Thirdly, my banker friend tells me that you're in a much better position in settling a dispute by using a credit card rather than a debit card. Again, the money at risk is the credit card company's, not yours, and a credit card company will more easily settle a dispute in your favor than your bank.

A case in point: Several years ago, I bought a piece of software on eBay. I should

have known that the price was too good to be true. The disk I got wasn't an original copy, and it wouldn't operate on my computer. I reported it to my bank at the time, and my account was credited for the transaction, pending settlement of the dispute.

Fortunately, the merchant agreed to refund my money if I returned the disk, which I did.

However, my banker friend told me that if the merchant hadn't been willing to refund the money, I probably would have lost it because I had legitimately ordered the software, using my debit card. Had I used a credit card, the issuer would have most likely taken the hit, he said.

If you make a lot of purchases online, it may make sense to have a credit card just for those purchases.

I have a friend who maintains a separate bank account and debit card just for online purchases. When he wants to buy something online, he puts just that much money in the account, so anyone stealing his identity will find nothing more to steal.

Based on what my banker friend told me, that could be more easily accomplished with a credit card.

My banker friend advised to only get one without an annual fee and only charge anything with the understanding that you'll immediately pay it off once you get the bill.

Letting a $10 charge languish for a couple of months is the worst thing you can do, he added. That can quickly ruin your credit, he said.

CHAPTER 6

Building a budget helps keep your plan afloat

Break this complicated task into smaller, more-manageable parts to make it easier to do

For a long time I had trouble budgeting. I felt overwhelmed trying to remember all the things that I needed to include. When I thought I had finally created a reasonable budget, something unexpected would blow the whole thing up. I finally did what one should with all complex tasks: Break it down into smaller, more manageable parts.

Once you have decided to live more frugally so you can save for emergencies and pay off debt as quickly as possible, and you've set some goals and priorities, you'll need to keep track of how well your plan is working. That's the purpose of the budget.

Like me, I believe many people shy away from making a monthly budget because they let complexity get the better of them.

I started with the easiest categories to budget and worked my way down to the hardest, using several concepts I learned in my college economics and accounting classes: fixed costs and variable costs.

In the business world, fixed costs are those you need to pay no matter what, like the costs of renting or owning a building. Variable costs will go up as you do more business. As you make more widgets, you'll need more raw materials and to pay more wages, for example.

I also reasoned that I had regular costs, those that occur every month, and those that occur periodically or unexpectedly.

After totaling all expected income for the month, I divided my expenses into four categories: **regular fixed expenses, regular variable expenses, irregular fixed and irregular variable.**

To do the same, start by figuring your monthly income: take-home pay plus any other income that you'll use to pay bills.

Regular fixed expenses are the easiest to budget because these are ones with set amounts that you have to pay every month, like your mortgage or rent, utilities and car payments.

I strongly recommend budget billing, so you pay about the same amount every month, and direct debit such items as utilities and auto, home and other insurance payments.

I've noticed that my budget-billed insurance and utility payments aren't always the same each month; they'll change by a few dollars. The gas bill has even gone from a low of $36 to a high of $66 per month. But that's still better than getting the shock of going from $15 per month in the summer to $150 or more in the winter. And the statements come before the start of the month, so you can easily plug the amounts into your monthly budget.

Fixed expenses that you pay quarterly or every six months should be divided into monthly installments and recorded here as well.

Also include regular church support. **Pay God first.**

After totaling all your regular fixed expenses, subtract them from your income to see how much you have left to budget.

Regular variable expenses are the second-easiest to budget. Although they will vary, they probably won't vary by much each month. After several months of record keeping, you'll be able to estimate them fairly closely. Examples are groceries and gasoline for daily transportation. Although they will go up and down, they probably won't vary widely; you won't eat $100 in food one month, $1,000 the next, or drive 1,000 miles one month, 10,000 the next.

If you're also trying to save a set amount each month for something special, like Christmas spending or future purchases, this is a good category in which to record it.

Again, total your regular variable expenses and subtract that from the income you had left after subtracting your regular fixed expenses.

Irregular fixed expenses are the hardest to budget because these occur periodically—or crop up unexpectedly—like car repairs and doctor visits. But by this point, you'll also have a relatively small

A model of the Titanic strikes an iceberg at the Titanic Museum in Pigeon Forge, Tenn.

"Beware of small expenses; a small hole can sink a great ship."

— BENJAMIN FRANKLIN

amount of income left to budget and a small number of categories, which should make the task easier.

Budgeting for these items is mainly a task of allocating a reasonable amount for car repairs, medical expenses and like items from the remaining income not budgeted.

I budget about $300 each for car repairs and medical bills each month, knowing if I don't need that this month, I'll probably need $600 next month or $900 the month after that. And, of course, I've seen expenses go over budget. It may take a year to track such expenses to get a good handle on how much to allocate each month.

This is also a good place for a miscellaneous line item to catch the small expenses that crop up and don't fit nicely somewhere else.

Again, total these allocated amounts and subtract them from the remaining income to be budgeted.

Irregular variable expenses are mainly discretionary spending— what you have left for yourself after you've met your regular expenses and allocated enough to cover irregular fixed expenses. This includes restaurants, movies, other entertainment and pocket money.

If you get down to this category and you're out of money, there'll be no discretionary spending this month. Or you may need to squeeze something in the above categories to get a little spending money.

If you don't have enough…

One of the values of this approach is that you can see after each step how much money you have left and can readily determine if you'll have enough for the remaining categories.

If you don't have enough to reasonably allocate some money for unexpected expenses, you need to trim something above.

If you won't have enough money left after paying regular fixed expenses to reasonably cover everything else, you'll know that you either need more income, a less-expensive place to live or a cheaper car to drive. This is when Dave Ramsey often tells his radio listeners to "sell the car," or homeowners discover that they're "house poor" because they bought too expensive a house. They face not only high house payments but higher taxes, higher insurance and more upkeep than they would have on a more affordable home.

To help you determine whether you're overspending on certain budget categories, I've included percentage guidelines for the main categories in the Simplified Zero-Balance Budget form that ends this chapter. These are averaged from several guidelines, one by the Michigan Counseling Association,[1] and the second by another author and friend, Larry Perry.[2] Note these are not hard-and-fast rules but just guidelines as to how much you should be spending.

If you're within 5 percent on the categories, you're probably OK, but note that the Simplified Zero-Balance Budget already suggests spending 55 percent of your income on regular fixed expenses and another 20 percent on regular variable expenses, including food and operating automobiles. That only leaves 25 percent for unexpected expenses and discretionary spending.

If you want more money for unexpected costs that pop up, or more discretionary spending, you need to lower your regular fixed and variable expenses. The main ways to do that are to pay off debt ASAP and avoid overspending on housing or automobiles.

Found money

One question that comes up is what to do with "found money" that you find left over at the end of the month because you were able to stay within the budget. My advice is to allocate found money toward next month's irregular fixed expenses or put it toward whatever step you're on in your financial plan.

If you don't have a starter emergency fund, put it toward that. If you're striving to pay off debt, put it toward that. If you're striving to build a full emergency fund, put it toward that.

Once you achieve those goals, you've got some breathing room. You could then choose to treat yourself. But, consider the opportunity cost of doing so. You could also put found money toward achieving other goals: paying off your house early, putting more toward retirement or more quickly reaching one of your bucket list goals.

It bears repeating that the purpose of the budget is to make sure you stay on track as you build your emergency fund, pay off debt, and save for both routine purchases as well as those cherished items on your bucket list.

This form will help you create a simplified zero-balance budget

List monthly income, then subtract known expenses you must pay. Then subtract other estimated expenses, and finally discretionary spending until you reach zero. Percentages suggest what you should spend in each category.

Income:

Salary or hourly wages for month ____________

Interest income on savings ____________

Investment income ____________

Other income: ____________

__________________________ ____________

__________________________ ____________

Total income for month ____________

Fixed costs (set amounts due monthly):

Church support (5%) ____________

Housing (30%)
    Mortgage payment/rent ____________
    Homeowners'/renters' insurance ____________
    Homeowners' association dues ____________
    Lawn care ____________
    Pest control ____________
    Utilities:
        Gas ____________
        Electricity ____________
        Water & sewer ____________
        Garbage pickup ____________

Automobile ownership (10%)
    Payments ____________

Insurance ____________

License/taxes ____________

Other ____________

Other insurance (5%)
    Life ____________
    Health ____________
    Long-term disability ____________
    Umbrella liability ____________
    Identity theft ____________

Debt repayment (5%)
    Loans and notes ____________
    Credit cards ____________
    Other ____________

Other fixed cost

__________________________ ____________

__________________________ ____________

Total fixed costs ____________

Remaining income to budget ____________

Regular variable costs (usual expenses that vary)

Food/groceries (15%) ____________

Daily transportation/gasoline (5%) ____________

Other charitable giving (5%) _____________

Savings for future purchases (5%)
   Car replacement _____________
   Other future purchases:

   _________________________ _____________

   _________________________ _____________

Beauty/barber shop _____________

Laundry/dry cleaning _____________

Children's school lunches/activities _____________

Other regular variable cost:

   _________________________ _____________

   _________________________ _____________

Total regular variable costs _____________

Remaining income to budget _____________

Irregular fixed expenses (occasional or unexpected)

Medical expenses (5%)
   Doctors/dentists _____________
   Drugs _____________

Miscellaneous (5%)
   Clothing _____________
   Cosmetics _____________
   Pocket money _____________
   Other _____________

Gifts (including Christmas) _____________

Car repairs (Included in auto %) _____________

Home repairs (Included in home %) _____________

Taxes
   Income _____________
   Property _____________
   Other taxes _____________

Other irregular fixed expenses:

   _________________________ _____________

   _________________________ _____________

Total irregular fixed costs _____________

Remaining income to budget _____________

Irregular variable expenses (discretionary spending)

Entertainment/recreation (5%)
   Restaurants _____________
   Books/movies _____________
   Baby-sitters _____________
   Vacation _____________
   Other:

   _________________________ _____________

   _________________________ _____________

Total irregular variable costs _____________

Remainder (should be zero) _____________

Fog envelops the John Oliver cabin on a Fall morning in Great Smoky Mountains National Park.

"Be it ever so humble, there's no place like home."

— "HOME! SWEET HOME!" JOHN HOWARD PAYNE AND SIR HENRY BISHOP

CHAPTER 7

Trust God to lead you to your earthly home

Seek His guidance when you're buying real estate

In 1993, my business partner put me on to a deal that was too good to pass up.

Several times, he'd urged me to buy a house with an apartment as a way to make money as well as have a place to live; I could live in the apartment and rent out the rest of the house.

But I resisted. I'm neither handy with home repairs nor was I interested in doing yard work. And I'd heard plenty of horror stories about tenants. I really didn't want the headaches of finding and keeping good tenants who wouldn't tear up my property.

Ever since getting out of college 20 years earlier, I'd rented. Being single and having no dependents, I saw no need to own a house. Following the advice of my frugal mother, I found good deals renting basement or second-story apartments in private homes. These landlords didn't charge top dollar, and they seemed happy to have a stable tenant. These were good deals for both of us.

However, when my partner told me that I could buy a duplex for $27,000, it piqued my interest. It was an old commercial building that had been added onto at the rear (It looked like two mobile homes attached end-to-end). It had been converted into two apartments by a plumber, so we knew the plumbing and heating plant had been properly installed.

Better yet, a retired engineer lived in one apartment, and he wanted to stay.

Even better still, after putting $11,000 down and borrowing $16,000, the engineer's rent made my mortgage payment, with a few dollars left over to put toward upkeep, taxes and insurance.

And shortly after the purchase, the previous owners told me where I could find a used Maytag washer and dryer for $100.

Because this deal was so good, I knew God was looking out for me, and the reason for His beneficence was revealed soon afterward. About nine months later, my 92-year-old mother needed to move from her home into an assisted-living apartment, and I needed a place for my belongings that I'd left in her basement over the years.

There are several lessons one can learn from this experience:

• If you don't need to own, there's nothing wrong with renting.

• Buying a duplex or a home in which you can rent an apartment is a good way to buy your first home.

• God loves you and will take care of you if you accept His guidance.

Rent vs. own

There are pros and cons to both renting and owning.

Even though the rent paid my mortgage, I figured my monthly costs for insurance, property taxes and upkeep still exceeded the $125 per month rent I'd been paying. That was for a second-story apartment in a 1900s farmhouse a couple of blocks away.

So don't assume it's always less expensive to own than rent. As my banker friend told me, in any situation like this, do the math!

Although it's often better to put money towards building equity than paying rent, you also need to consider how much home ownership will cost you in taxes, homeowners' association fees, monthly upkeep, insurance and the anticipated costs of replacing major appliances and the roof.

As in my situation above, you might find it cheaper to rent.

And if you don't want the responsibility of a home, you're only going to live in an area for a short time, or you travel a lot and won't be home to take care of the property, there's nothing wrong with renting.

And if you can rent less expensively than you can own, putting the money you save into good mutual funds will probably earn you more in the long run than you will realize in a house's appreciation.

But having said that, it's great to have something that's yours and you can do with as you see fit. I love my present home, even though it—at least initially—cost me more than renting would have.

Being an owner/landlord

Being an owner/landlord was a good experience, although it was challenging at times.

My tenant was supposed to take care of the yard in exchange for a discount on his rent but he dawdled, and the grass grew high.

I raised his rent and took over the chore until I determined that I didn't have the time or ambition for it. So I hired a neighbor kid to mow the yard, and I trimmed hard-to-get-to areas with a push mower.

When my tenant's refrigerator went out, I had to replace it.

And after moving to Tennessee, while I still owned the duplex, I was told it had termites, which I had to take care of while living far away.

But for the most part, I had a good tenant, and after making some improvements to the property, I sold it for my asking price of $40,000, which was about $8,000 more than what I had put into it.

Fortunately, I'd found a good real estate agent to serve as a property manager when I couldn't sell the property for what I wanted before leaving.

Within two years, she found a buyer who was willing to pay my asking price.

A woman friend of mine, who was divorced at the time, also rented out her lower level to help make ends meet. She echoed my belief: "God always seemed to send me what I needed."

The duplex was a godsend, and it was a good investment over the eight years that I owned it before moving to Tennessee.

'God will pay the freight'

From 1988, I'd felt the urge to move on.

That led me to pursue a master's degree in journalism from the University of Missouri-Columbia from 1989–1991 with the hope that I would be able to advance in my chosen profession.

After a post-graduate job hunting trip through the South, which included two interviews in Knoxville and a side trip to Cades Cove in Great Smoky Mountains National Park, I fell in love with East Tennessee and believed that that's where I was being called to live.

However, I remained in Iowa during my mother's final years; she passed away in 1998.

And I wondered if I was really being called to Tennessee or whether I was just seeking "greener grass on the other side of the fence".

A woman I knew from church, who was a missionary in Haiti, told me Haitians had a saying: "If God wants you to move, He will pay the freight."

Several weeks later, at a party, I shared my desire to move to Tennessee with an acquaintance who drove an 18-wheeler.

He volunteered to move me, telling me he'd load my furniture and my two collector cars into a trailer and that I could ride up front with him.

God, indeed, was arranging my move to the foothills of East Tennessee.

Another Godsend

After dealing with the maintenance of an old building and accompanying yard work, I knew I wanted a recently built condominium with minimum maintenance—and someone else taking care of the yard work.

Looking at properties online, I found an all-brick, two-story condo that piqued my interest, and called the real-estate agent who had the property listed.

On a subsequent house-hunting trip, she showed me a number of properties around Knoxville and Maryville, and we ended up at the one I'd seen online.

I soon decided that the two-story home was much more than what I needed or wanted.

But I liked the subdivision, and I remembered my brother Milo's prescription for making money in real estate: "Go to the nicest neighborhood and buy the least expensive house."

So when we got back to her office, I asked her to look up the lowest-priced condo listed in the development. She found a new listing.

I wasn't able to look at it then but I did on another trip.

By then another condo around the corner was up for sale, and we looked at it first.

"I could live here," Linda said. When we next toured the condo I'd intended to see, she changed her mind. "I want this one."

She has since told me that if I ever want to sell it, I should let her know.

But when I went to make an offer, I discovered that another party had a first option; I would be making a backup offer.

To give this my best shot, I went to the county property assessor to discover comparable sales in the neighborhood. From that I computed a $135,500 counteroffer to the $139,900 asking price.

My offer was accepted, in part because the party with the first option failed to exercise it by their deadline. I later learned through my agent that they were willing to pay me the full asking price if I were willing to sell. But I loved the house; I wanted to keep it, and I still do.

Pay off the mortgage early

When you do buy a home, **enter into no longer than a 15-year mortgage, and strive to pay it off early**.

You'll discover that your payment on a 30-year mortgage isn't much lower than a 15-year mortgage but you'll pay a lot more interest over a 30-year loan.[1]

And you'll save even more if you pay extra principal throughout the life of the loan.

Making just one extra payment each year by adding one-twelfth to your monthly payment is easy, and I was able to pay off a 15-year mortgage in a little under 13 years. How to do so is explained in the accompanying sidebar.

Of course, if you can afford more than an extra twelfth per month, add as much onto the monthly mortgage payment as you can. Remaining interest is computed on the unpaid balance of the loan. The sooner the unpaid balance goes down, the less interest you'll pay.

And if you find extra money—such as a bonus or a tax refund— apply that to pay off the mortgage even faster and save more interest.

Do not sign up for a biweekly "accelerator" payment program. It

Try this alternative to a biweekly payment to pay off a mortgage early

Theoretically, an easy way to pay off a mortgage early is to make half payments every two weeks. With 52 weeks in a year, you make 26 half payments, the equivalent of 13 months' full payments. For example, if you had a $1,200 monthly payment on a 15-year loan, $14,400 yearly, you would pay $600 every two weeks, $15,600 in a year.

In all but two months of the year, you'd pay the same amount as before; for the other two months, you'd make an extra half payment.

The idea is it's easy to do but will bring down the interest more quickly because interest is calculated on the loan's unpaid balance.

However, I learned through painful experience that signing up for my bank's program, whereby I made half payments every two weeks, didn't accelerate the mortgage payments.

Instead, the bank's subsidiary that offered this "service" held the first half-payment until it received the second, then applied it all just like a regular monthly mortgage payment.

The bank's subsidiary essentially got a short-term loan from me, for which they charged a service fee and paid a pittance of interest on the money that was held for two weeks.

I only discovered this after I tried to set up my own two-week payment when online bill payment became available through my bank. I was told by the company holding the loan that it didn't accept biweekly payments.

A little Internet research showed that this is common practice among these programs.[2]

Biweekly loan payments only benefit you if your lender will credit your payment and recalculate the interest and outstanding balance every two weeks. A true biweekly loan has to be set up that way, and few lenders offer them.[3]

To accomplish much the same thing with monthly payments, add one-twelfth to the payment with the extra specified to be principal reduction.

Following the example above, you would add $100 (one-twelfth of $1,200), to pay $1,300 monthly, $15,600 yearly. The principal will be reduced, and interest on the outstanding balance will be recalculated each month.

In 12 years, you'll have made 13 years' payments, one of which is all principal reduction. Within another year, you'll have paid off the loan.

sounds great in theory but it doesn't work in practice. That too is explained in the accompanying sidebar.

Make a balloon payment

With new higher standard deductions, you probably won't have enough itemized deductions to justify taking a mortgage-interest deduction but if you do, you'll reach a point (I did after about 10 years) that there isn't enough interest left to pay to justify taking a tax deduction.

If you haven't already paid off the mortgage by then, this is a good time to make a balloon payment, paying off the remaining principal balance in a lump sum.

That's because when you first take out a mortgage, your monthly payment is primarily interest with just a tiny bit of principal repayment. As you go through the life of the loan, you will pay steadily less interest and more principal until, near the end of the loan, you're paying back mostly principal and little interest.

So near the end of the loan, there's not enough mortgage interest being paid to make much of a difference in your tax bill.

Therefore, you should pay off the remaining principal balance as soon as you can afford to do so and save the remaining interest you would otherwise pay.

Mortgage moral: Trust in God

When good opportunities present themselves, and everything works out right, that's a sure sign that God is with you in your venture.

He was with me in buying my first home, becoming an owner/landlord and in finding me a new home in Tennessee.

On the other hand, if what you want to do isn't working, that's a good sign that it isn't meant to be.

So you should consult with God before making any important life decision, including purchasing a home, which will be one of your biggest life purchases.

What proved to be a great opportunity for me might not be so for you.

A Maryville, Tennessee, home displays the U.S. flag.

"…and your house will be my home as long as I live."

— PSALMS 23:6, GOOD NEWS BIBLE

CHAPTER 8

Learn to become a cultivator of wealth

Love what you do, but make it work for you

Throughout my newspaper career, I enjoyed making a difference through reporting information that my readers wanted or needed to know.

Starting with a love of photography, I learned to write so I could get paid for both.

As I went along, I learned the power of combining words and photos, each reinforcing the other, the idea that one and one can equal more than two.

To further accomplish that, I became interested in page design to present the words and pictures in compelling ways.

It was a great career for a journalist with a visual bent, and as I went along, I moved from conveying information that my readers wanted or found interesting to trying to convey ideas I felt strongly about.

One of my most satisfying projects was promoting the idea of a scenic byway though the part of Eastern Iowa where I lived.

I drove my 1966 Ford Mustang convertible along the route, photographing the sights and writing about them, taking readers along through successive pages of a tourism tabloid that our company published.

I subsequently editorialized about how such a route could promote development throughout the area just before the governor was to visit. I made sure his office received a copy of the editorial beforehand.

That effort—as well as the intervention of our state representative—I'm sure helped make the scenic byway a reality.

But writing for a newspaper has a major drawback. Once it is published, an article's useful life is only a day or a week.

Afterward, it will be thrown out, and the journalist needs to start all over again on another report. You can't inventory your work for later resale. But a book hopefully will have a much longer shelf life.

The ideas are more timeless than timely, the photographs and matching quotations have a longer appeal, and from an economic perspective, an author can (again, hopefully) sell his book over and over again for years.

And the material can be updated relatively easily into a new edition, further extending its sales life.

Hunter-gatherer vs. cultivator

Most career advisers will recommend that you do what you love because you'll spend more time with it, you will get better at it, you will be more enthusiastic about it, and you will be willing to do the necessary research into what you'll need to do to prepare for what your career will demand.

But Dr. Stanley, author of *The Millionaire Next Door* series, also noted in his third book of the series, fifth book overall, *Millionaire Women Next Door*, that successful millionaire entrepreneurs have also learned to become cultivators of wealth, as opposed to being hunter-gatherers.[1]

He noted that back in prehistoric days, hunter-gatherers, usually the men of the tribe, had to go out and "kill something and drag it back to the cave," as Dave Ramsey would say, or gather wild berries, apples or whatever else was in season in order to eat—a task that became more difficult as winter came on and as the hunter-gatherers became older.

The women, who stayed back at the camp to bear and raise children, learned to plant seeds and cultivate them, and were able to harvest crops that could be eaten all season long. Eventually, they learned ways to preserve what they harvested to last them over the long winter.

Today, many are still hunter-gatherers in that they have to do something every day, such as sell something or work a shift, in order to survive, while modern-day cultivators, like authors, software developers and investors, put their work into products like books and computer programs that can be sold over and over for many years, or investments that will yield growth and/or dividends for years to come.

The trick is to find a way to take your God-given skills and create "seeds" that you can plant and cultivate for future growth.

Brian's story

Stanley, in *Millionaire Women Next Door*, devotes a chapter to Brian, a successful young man who wrote to the author about how he went from being a modern-day hunter-gatherer to becoming a cultivator of wealth.[2]

I love this story because it speaks to anyone who might want to start his or her own business, especially in retailing.

A dyslexic high school student, Brian didn't do well academically.

But he loved cars and got a job working in a car wash, soon advancing to detailing cars. He loved his job and was so good at it that customers specifically asked for him to do their detailing.

Following school, he decided to start his own auto detailing business and, according to Stanley's account, appeared to do everything right.

He started by surveying his would-be customers on where they would like to have their cars detailed. He determined that it would be at their homes. So he went to them, saving himself the cost of renting a shop.

When he realized he could only detail so many cars in a week, and that he couldn't delegate his passion for doing exceptionally fine work, he specialized in detailing high-end cars, for which his customers would pay a premium, and he moved to the city that had the highest proportion of highly expensive cars in the country.

Successful millionaires have learned to become cultivators of wealth, as opposed to being hunter-gatherers.

— DR. THOMAS J. STANLEY,
MILLIONAIRE WOMEN NEXT DOOR

Still, Brian was a hunter-gatherer.

Even though his success enabled him to live in a nice home and to buy a motorcycle and several fine cars, he still had to go to work every day in order to keep up his income and corresponding lifestyle.

His epiphany came when one of his wealthy customers told Brian that he wouldn't be needed that week, because the customer and his wife were going to Hawaii.

They didn't return for three weeks; the weather was so nice that they decided to stay another two weeks.

"I could never in my business just decide to take off 'another two weeks'," Brian wrote

to Stanley. "I have scheduled commitments … impossible."[3]

So how could put himself in such a position?

Being a student of his clients' lifestyles, he noted many doctors and lawyers were never at home; they were always working no matter how early or late he showed up.

But many others owned apartment buildings and always had time to talk to him. He sought advice from those wealthy clients who were happy to share their insights.

Buy a four-plex apartment building, live in one and rent out the others, one told him; sell your big house and toys until you're wealthy; only then buy them back, said another.

Starting with one four-plex and the proceeds from his auto detailing business, Brian went on to buy the one next door, and another, and another.

He still detailed cars because he loved doing so, according to Stanley, but Brian's wealth came from his apartment business, which paid him whether he was working or not.

By the time the book was written in 2004, Brian had written:

"Today at age 41, I still live in the same two-bedroom four-plex I started with, and my estate is over $5 million. [I have a] net worth near $2 million. In about two more weeks, I will have about 250 tenants … all in four-plexes. I bought both four-plexes on both sides of mine … and so on …"[4]

Farmers cut oats using antique implements in Iowa County, Iowa.

"We derive our dignity from earning our daily bread."

— POPE FRANCIS

Two approaches to car sales

Perhaps today's most stereotypical hunter-gatherer is the car salesperson. He may have a sales quota to meet, so he's eager to sell you a car now.

One time while looking for a used car, I walked onto a lot and was approached by a salesperson who seemed determined to sell me something that day even though he didn't have what I wanted: a two-door hatchback with a stick shift that would get good mileage and be inexpensive to buy and own.

Because the same company owned several nearby dealerships, he drove me around to most of them and tried to interest me in what he could find, none of which was what I was looking for. I gave him a fairly complete description of what I wanted, including several models that I thought I'd like. He promised to get back to me if he found something but never did.

At another time during the same car search, I asked a prominent businessman friend for a recommendation as to who could help me find what I was looking for.

He referred me to a salesman he dealt with. This salesman had a four-door Saturn sedan he was trying to sell. I test drove it but decided it wasn't what I was looking for.

He was visibly disappointed that I was unwilling to buy this car. I again described what I was looking for, including several models I thought would work. I thought he could check his online sources. He seemed irritated as he wrote down my information.

I never heard back from him either.

Nor did I contact either of these salesmen again. I found a car that met my needs in the newspaper classifieds, which was offered by a private seller.

Next time I'll probably check Craigslist.

But it doesn't have to be that way. Also in *Millionaire Women Next Door*, Stanley devotes a chapter to Beverly, a car salesperson who became a millionaire by cultivating relationships.[5]

While the men around her were like the ones above, waiting for customers to come to them, Beverly was on the phone prospecting for customers. She maintained contacts with the great number of customers who had bought cars from her, to inquire about their current needs and ask for referrals.

On rainy days, she called businesses to see if they might need new vehicles. **She wanted to be the first person everyone thought of when they wanted to buy a car.**

Rather than advertising in traditional media, Beverly said, "I buy ads in everything the churches print!" She supported her own church as well as others.

"I sell to all the clergy at cost. No commission. I never want to make money off them," she said.

"A manager once said, 'You could have held back five hundred dollars on that trade you made with that minister.' I said, 'Not me, I'm not messing with God or any of His representatives'."[6]

She persuaded her managers to sell a late-model van at cost, with no commission, to a couple who had three children with Down's Syndrome, and who had adopted four more.

Months later, after the warranty had expired, the van developed a mechanical problem, necessitating an $1,800 repair.

"I went to the general manager and our bean counter [accountant] and said, 'We need to fix this, and we need to swallow it [no charge to the family for the repairs].' They said okay, called the service manager, and he repaired it at no charge."[7]

Serving the needs of others made Beverly a millionaire. According to Stanley, she regularly sold 250 to 275 cars a year.

As the second-place performer in a national sales contest, she was challenged by the luxury brand's senior vice president for America, who intimated she might not be in the top five the following year. In turn, she bet him $100 that she'd be the top performer in the year to come.

As the awards ceremony for that year neared, she got a congratulatory letter from the vice president, which contained a $100 bill, for she had sold 369 vehicles, better than one per day.[8]

When I was an undergraduate marketing major, I was introduced to The Marketing Concept,[9] the philosophy that to be successful, a business should first seek to determine its customers' needs, then seek to satisfy those needs.

It always seemed a common sense approach to me, an extension of the Golden Rule: Do unto others as you would have them do unto you.

Or, as Beverly herself put it:

"Too many salespeople forget that it's the customer who makes them what they are today … it's the customers … Always respect them. Always treat them right. Appreciate them. All of them." [10]

Cultivating in retailing

Do what you love in selecting a career, but also look for ways to become a cultivator of wealth rather than just being a hunter-gatherer.

I've thought that auto and home insurance agents may have great potential to become cultivators of wealth. One must develop a large client base, like car salesperson Beverly above, but once one does, he/she gains a steady stream of revenue from renewals.

Of course, one must provide good service and seek to replace customers who move away, die or otherwise leave, but having a steady income stream is a good precursor to wealth building.

When I shared this idea with an economic development professional, he added that in the case of car insurance, it immensely helps your sales pitch to be selling a product that the government says you must buy.

Many people who dream of owning their own business look to retailing, but Stanley presents statistics in *Millionaire Women Next Door* that show retail businesses have one of the lowest profit margins of any business category.

"Overall, the retail trade accounts for only 5.5 percent of all profits (net income) generated by all small business establishments in America." [11]

And it's no wonder.

Most retail establishments have high up-front costs: If you're a brick-and-mortar retailer, you must rent a storefront and refurbish it as needed, buy merchandise—usually with borrowed money—and advertise your offerings to potential customers.

Then you have to hope to get enough customers to come in and buy enough merchandise to offset those costs, as well as hope they don't steal from you or return the merchandise.

And today, you must compete with online retailers, from which you can buy almost anything and have it delivered to your door.

As a photographer, I've printed, matted and framed some of my best pieces from the Great Smoky Mountains and have tried to sell them through several arts and crafts shops in Townsend, Tenn., just outside Great Smoky Mountains National Park.

I figured many of the millions of tourists that flock to the park might like a nicer souvenir than much of the kitsch that is found in typical souvenir shops.

I was wrong.

Fortunately, I started with just a few offerings. I sold a couple to a framing shop, and placed a dozen or so photos with an arts-and-crafts consignment shop. Out of that group, I sold one.

Other artists apparently had not much more success than I did, because those shops went out of business not long afterward.

But as I researched those shops, I found one business model that appeared to be profitable because it seemed to employ Stanley's idea of wealth cultivation.

That was a shop that was divided into a number of booths, each operated by a different artist or craftsperson.

The shop owner told me each booth holder paid him rent plus a percentage of the sales made.

I understand some antique shops are organized the same way; the shop is divided into booths that are rented out to individual dealers, who also pay a percentage of each sale made to the shop owner.

If I were going into such a venture, I'd want to be the shop owner.

It seems to me that he has the best opportunity to make money. That's because he has a built-in revenue stream from the booth rental, regardless of whether any merchandise sells.

He will also collect a percentage on all merchandise sold.

And if he likes or sells antiques, he is in the best position to shop what other booth holders bring in for sale.

Cultivating investments

I hope you see the pattern; you want to get away from having to repeat the same tasks every day—even if you love them—to make a living.

Rather, you want to create a situation where money regularly comes to you, such as through Brian's rental properties, Beverly's long list of customers who think of her when they need a car, or my trying to write a book that will hopefully sell for years.

Even if your career choice doesn't present a good opportunity to cultivate wealth, you can still do so through saving and investing, which is how I did so before I decided to write this book.

Again, Stanley, this time in his second book, *The Millionaire Mind*, tells the story of Mr. Benjamin, a school bus driver who generated enough income to send his children to private colleges, medical school and graduate school.

"He was frugal, but being frugal is not enough to pay for six-figure tuition bills,"[12] Stanley wrote.

Realizing when they were young that his children were very bright and would benefit from a top-flight education, Mr. Benjamin fretted over how he could give them that kind of education on his meager school bus driver's salary.

One side benefit he had was several hours of downtime each school day. While other bus drivers whiled away their time sleeping, chatting or reading newspapers and magazines, Mr. Benjamin began a focused reading program, centering on investments.

Early into his studies, he concluded that after adjusting for inflation and taxes, only stocks paid a real return on one's investment dollars over the long term.

Eventually, he became a serious stock investor, concentrating in the stock offerings of specific corporations, which he'd investigated through his reading program.

When he retired, the former bus driver had a net worth of over $3 million. Stanley noted that was after he'd sent his children to the best schools in America.[13]

Not everyone may have the time or inclination to research investments like Mr. Benjamin.

But there are investment strategies that anyone can follow.

It may not be child's play, but as you'll see in the next chapter, it's not rocket science either.

46

A farmer moves soybeans to a wagon in Iowa County, Iowa.

Find a way to take your God-given skills and create "seeds" you can plant and cultivate for future growth.

CHAPTER 9

Concentrate on what you have control over

Use simple strategies as you invest for retirement and children's college

I was looking forward to retirement in 2007. I was 57 on October 12, and I planned to retire in five years, at age 62. My investments were doing well. By that October, my portfolio balance had reached a high of over $600,000. I figured if I averaged 10 percent per year—not including compound interest, I'd have over $1 million in five years' time, my retirement goal.

Then it started declining.

By October 2008, the bottom dropped out.

By the end of March 2009, just after the stock market hit rock-bottom; my portfolio total stood at just over $330,000. It was down by roughly 48 percent.

What does one do when one's investments drop by nearly half?

I knew enough not to sell out. But I wondered what—if anything—I could do to help my situation.

Then, I read an article, "Five Ways to Fix Up Your 401(k) Plan" in the *Wall Street Journal Sunday,* a personal finance section that appeared in the *Knoxville News-Sentinel*. Among the advice it offered for rebuilding one's portfolio after such a downturn was to bump up your 401(k) plan contribution.[1]

I recognized a good idea when I saw it. I knew from history that the stock market would rise again.

I reasoned that other than for housing and the sub-prime mortgage market, the U.S. economy was fundamentally sound, and it would come back. The only question was when.

Save for retirement with these plans

Workplace retirement plans: Contributions to these tax-deferred savings plans (named for the tax code sections that authorize them) are not taxed when you make them, and they grow with taxes deferred; you don't pay tax until you withdraw the proceeds, which you usually can do at age 59-1/2 and which you must now do by age 73; This age will rise to 75 in the future.

401(k) plans are used by private employers.

403(b) plans are used by schools, hospitals and other non-profit organizations.

457 plans are used by state and local governments.

The Thrift Savings Plan is used by the federal government.

For all the plans above, yearly contribution limits as of 2024 are $23,000 if you're under 50, $30,500 if over 50.[2]

SIMPLE plans are available to self-employed persons. Yearly contribution limits as of 2024 are $16,000 if you're under 50, $19,500 if over 50.[3]

Roth 401(k) plans are offered by some employers. Unlike the plans above, you pay tax on your contributions but they grow tax-free, and withdrawals, which usually can start without penalty at age 59-1/2, are tax-free. And there's no mandatory withdrawal. Yearly contribution limits as of 2024 are $23,000 if you're under 50, $30,500 if over 50.[4]

Individual plans: Use these if you don't have one available at work.

Individual Retirement Accounts are like the employer-sponsored plans above; contributions to a traditional IRA are tax-deferred until withdrawn, which you can start doing without penalty at age 59-1/2 and you must now do by age 73. This age will rise to 75 in the future.

Roth IRAs are like Roth 401(k)s. You pay tax on the money that goes into the plan but it grows tax-free, and withdrawals are tax-free. And there's no mandatory withdrawal.

Yearly contribution limits as of 2024 are $7,000 if you're under 50, $8.000 if over 50. for both IRAs.[5]

I thought to contribute another 5 percent to my 401(k) plan but I wondered if I could I afford to do that?

As you may recall from previous chapters, I'm a natural saver, and I had a hard time budgeting.

Until then.

The prospect of adding to my 401(k) contribution while the stock market was likely at a lifetime low spurred me to get serious about budgeting.

I determined that, yes, I could add another 5 percent to the 20 percent of my salary I was already contributing.

"Think you can't save any more? Ask your payroll manager to calculate what your paycheck would look like if you boosted your 401(k) contribution," suggests Christine Benz, director of personal finance at investment research firm Morningstar.

"The percentages might seem daunting, but if you look at it in dollars-and-cents terms, you might find it's something you could easily implement," says Ms. Benz.[6]

And it paid off.

I was teaching about investments on March 9, 2010, one year to the day from when the stock market bottomed. As I told the class, the money I'd put in at the market bottom had gained nearly 70 percent in that year; the S&P 500 stock index had risen 69 percent.

By March 11, 2011, the S&P 500 was up 103 percent from its low, and by March 13, 2014, it was up 176 percent.[7] That's a 35 percent yearly average, a good return on a five-year investment.

And by March 9, 2017, eight years to the day after the stock market bottom, the S&P 500 was up 250 percent.[8] That's an average 31 percent yearly gain.

Daisies grow in Great Smoky Mountains National Park's Cades Cove.

"Notice how the flowers grow. They do not toil or spin. But I tell you, not even Solomon in all his splendor was dressed like one of them. If God so clothes the grass of the field that grows today and is thrown into the oven tomorrow, will He not much more provide for you?"
— Luke 12: 27-28

Control what you can control

Investments go up and down in value, and it's next to impossible to time the stock market with any degree of certainty. But there are several things that you can do.

The first—and most important—is to decide how much of your income to save.

When I was younger, the rule of thumb was to save 10 percent. However, as noted above, with no more knowledge of the subject than that, I decided in my late 20s that I wanted to be ahead of the curve. So I decided to save 20 percent yearly, which I tried to do every year afterward.

Due to inflation, my advice now is to save *at least* 15 percent of your income, more if you can. You may need to start with a lesser percentage, but work up to 15 percent or more.

Remember April and Ben in the first chapter? The moral was to **start saving as soon as you can, and save as much as you can for as long as you can**.

If you can't start with 15 percent, Vanguard—a mutual-fund company in which I have money invested—recommends starting where you can and adding 1 percent per year until you reach 12-15 percent.[9]

Second, you can decide where to save.

Start with your tax-favored retirement plan at work if you have one.

If you don't, or if you've maxed it out, next save in your own IRA. Use a Roth IRA if you believe you'll have more than $700,000 in retirement savings.[10]

Many firms offering tax-favored

Save for college with these plans

529 plans are educational savings accounts run by states or educational institutions to help families save for college. You pay tax on funds contributed but earnings are tax-free when used for qualified educational expenses. Plans differ, and many states allow contributions totaling $300,000. Beneficiaries can be changed; you can even set one up for yourself.[11]

Coverdell Educational Savings Accounts are more limited than 529 plans; you can only contribute $2,000 per year per child through age 18, but tax-free proceeds can be used for qualifying K-12 educational expenses as well as for college. Proceeds must be used before the beneficiary turns 30, but the beneficiary can be changed and remaining funds can be moved to a 529 plan.[12]

---

retirement plans, which are described in an accompanying box, have offered 50 or 100 percent matches on the first 2 to 6 percent you invest. That's free money, an immediate 50 or 100 percent return on your initial investment. It doesn't get better than that.

Even if your company has suspended the employer match, which many firms did following the 2008–2009 Great Recession, continue to invest in its retirement plan. The real benefit is that you don't pay tax on your investment until you take it out.

Simply put, if you are an average American family today, you make around $70,000 a year. If you save $10,500 in your company's tax favored retirement plan 15 percent—only $59,500 is subject to tax. Otherwise, it's the whole $70,000.

And the investment will grow tax-deferred until you take it out, which you can usually do, without penalty, at age 59-1/2, depending upon your employer's plan.

The Roth IRA and Roth 401(k) are different in that you pay tax on the funds you put in, but they grow tax-free, and you don't pay tax when you withdraw them.

So, if you believe you'll have substantial retirement savings—which would put you into a higher tax bracket then—a Roth IRA or Roth 401(k) (if you have one available at work) is a great investment vehicle.

For children's education, first consider a Coverdell Educational Savings Account, next a 529 plan. These are also described in an accompanying box.

And, of course, you'll want to have a bank or money market account for your emergency fund and bucket list items, perhaps a mutual fund account for those that are five years away or more.

Third, you can control the timing of your investments

If you're contributing to your retirement plan at work and put in the same amount each pay period, you're already using one good investment technique, perhaps without even knowing it: dollar cost averaging.

With the same amount invested each pay period, you buy more shares when prices are low and fewer shares when prices are high, which lowers your average cost per share.

This is a good default setting for investing, but you can also tweak it in high and low markets to gain even more shares for the same total cost.

A sidebar shows how this can work.

Fourth, you can control your investment costs

Different mutual funds have different costs, and you can control your investment costs primarily by choosing low-cost funds.

If you're investing in mutual funds on your own, one of the first costs you will encounter is a "load."

Some funds charge loads, which are sales commissions for the persons selling the funds. Conversely, those that don't charge such sales commissions are "no load" funds.

Studies vary on whether load funds or no-load funds perform better.[13] Therefore, as a general rule, you should avoid load funds.

However, there are good load funds, and a load is a one-time charge, so if you're planning to hold onto a fund for a long time, you shouldn't let a load deter you from an otherwise fine fund.

Even if a fund doesn't have a load, each has an "expense ratio," which includes "outlays for fund management, marketing, record keeping, administration, compliance and shareholder services. With many mutual funds, a 12b-1 fee, which covers a fund's marketing and distribution costs, makes up a large proportion of the expense ratio."[14]

The expense ratio is expressed as a percentage of your return, and is taken off before your return is reported to you. For example, if your fund grows by 12 percent in a year and it has a 1.5 percent expense ratio, you'll get 10.5 percent. (i.e., 12 − 1.5 = 10.5).

Also, because it's a percentage, as your returns compound, so does the expense ratio.

The U.S. Securities and Exchange Commission's investor.gov website notes:

Use Dollar Cost Averaging, Market Tweaks

The two calculations below show how dollar cost averaging works and how you can tweak your investments in low and high stock markets.

Let's imagine we're going to invest in a young drug company that is developing what they hope will be a promising new wonder drug. You decide to invest $1,000 per year over three years.

In what might be considered a "normal" market, the firm's price per share is $10 in Year 1, so your $1,000 buys100 shares.

By Year 2, initial drug tests don't looking promising. The stock's price per share has dropped to $5 per share—and your emotions are saying, "What have I done? Why did I buy this loser?"—but you believe in the company, so you stay the course, investing another $1,000, buying 200 shares.

By Year 3, clinical trials are going very well, and your emotions are screaming, "I should have bought more at $5!" But you stick to your plan and invest another $1,000, buying 50 shares.

As seen in the chart below, at left, by dollar cost averaging, you bought 350 shares for an average per-share price of $8.57, considerably lower than the average price of $11.67 over the three years.

| | **Dollar Cost Averaging** | | | | **Low-, High-Market Tweaks** | | |
Year	Invested	Price	#Shares		Invested	Price	#Shares
1.	$1,000	$10	100		$1,000	$10	100
2.	$1,000	$5	200		$1,100	$5	220
3.	$1,000	$20	50		$900	$20	45
	Total cost	Avg. price	#Shares		Total cost	Avg. price	#Shares
	$3,000	$11.67	350		$3,000	$11.67	365

Your average cost per share: $8.57 $8.22

Now let's imagine a second scenario: You're very confident of the success of our fictional drug company, so when its share price drops to $5 per share, you decide to bump up your investment by 10 percent to $1,100 and buy 220 shares, as shown in the chart above, at right. And when the price jumps to $20 per share, you realize $1,000 won't buy as much as it used to, so you decrease your investment by 10 percent, investing $900, buying 45 shares.

As a result, you bought 15 more shares for the same money than you would have with dollar cost averaging. Not bad.

"A fund with high costs must perform better than a low-cost fund to generate the same returns for you. Even small differences in fees can translate into large differences in returns over time. For example, if you invested $10,000 in a fund that produced a 5 percent annual return before expenses and had annual operating expenses of 1.5 percent, then after 20 years you would have roughly $19,612. But if the fund had expenses of only 0.5 percent, then you would end up with $24,002—a 23 percent difference.

*"It takes only minutes to use a mutual fund cost calculator such as FINRA's Fund Analyzer (*https://tools.finra.org/fund_analyzer/*) to compute how the costs of different mutual funds add up over time and eat into your returns."*[15]

A 2021 Investopedia article adds:

"A reasonable expense ratio for an actively managed portfolio is about 0.5 percent to 0.75 percent while an expense ratio greater than 1.5 percent is considered high these days.

"For passive or index funds, the typical ratio is about 0.2 percent but can be as low as 0.02 percent or less … ."[16]

Vanguard, as a case in point, is known for its very low fees.

First, it is a "mutual" mutual fund company. Like a mutual insurance company, its funds shareholders own the

"Even small differences in fees can translate into large differences in returns over time. For example, if you invested $10,000 in a fund that produced a 5 percent annual return before expenses and had annual operating expenses of 1.5 percent, then after 20 years you would have roughly $19,612. But if the fund had expenses of only 0.5 percent, then you would end up with $24,002—a 23 percent difference."

— U.S. Securities and Exchange Commission

company; it doesn't have stockholders looking for profits over and above its funds' shareholders. Nor does it have outside administrators.

Founder John C. Bogle explained his rationale in structuring the firm this way:

"Why should our mutual funds retain an outside company to manage their affairs—then, and now, the modus operandi *of our industry—when the funds could manage themselves and save a small fortune in fees."*[17]

And Vanguard's offerings are all no-load funds.[18]

Vanguard and Morningstar, Inc., noted that as of Dec. 31, 2022, the industry average expense ratio was 0.54 percent, where Vanguard's was 0.09 percent.[19]

An actively managed mutual fund will also charge transaction costs for buying and selling stock during the year, which are not disclosed. Bogle noted in his 1999 book:

"The costs that actively managed funds incur in buying and selling portfolio securities are hidden, but nonetheless real. Fund portfolio turnover averages some 80 percent annually. It is expensive, perhaps adding as much as 0.5 to 1.0 percentage points (or more) to the more visible cost of fund expenses."[20]

Vanguard offers actively managed funds, but is best known for its index funds. They invest in all of the stocks in a stock-market index and have much lower operating costs.

While managers of actively managed funds do a lot of costly research to decide on the stocks they believe will outperform the market, index fund managers just buy all the stocks in the index, in proportion to their weighting in the index.

One of its most popular is the Vanguard 500 Index fund, which invests in all the stocks of the S&P 500 Index and will be discussed further below.

A widely reported statistic is that index funds outperform most actively managed funds in their respective categories. For years, I thought that was because those active managers fail to do better than the market. But Bogle, who started the first publicly available index fund, noted in his 1999 book that costs make the difference:

"Over the past 15 years (1983-1998), the 16.0 percent return on the Wilshire 5000 Index exceeded the 14.1 percent net return on the average growth and value fund by 1.9 percentage points, precisely what we might have expected based on total estimated fund costs of 1.9 percent ... .[21]

"In fact, the lowest-cost publicly available index funds operate at annual expense ratios of less that 20/100 of 1 percent."[22]

While an actively managed U.S. stock fund may cost the investor 0.54 percent of his yearly return on average to pay for the aforementioned fees, the Vanguard 500 Index fund—for example—had an expense ratio of 0.14 percent as of April 28, 2023.[23]

And if you have more than $3,000 in the Vanguard 500 Index fund's Admiral shares,

"Most investors, both institutional and individual, will find that the best way to own common stocks is through an index fund that charges minimal fees."

— WARREN BUFFETT, BERKSHIRE HATHAWAY ANNUAL REPORT, 1996

your expense ratio drops to 0.04 percent.[23]

Therefore, if an actively managed fund and the Vanguard S&P 500 Index fund each earned 12 percent in a year, and the actively managed fund charged expenses of 0.54 percent, you would get a 11.46 percent return. With the Vanguard S&P 500 Index fund Admiral shares having a 0.04 expense ratio, you would earn 11.96 percent, one half of one percent more.

That may seem a small difference but it will add up over the 30 to 40 years you might be investing for retirement.

Even legendary investor Warren E. Buffett advocates index fund investing. In the 1996 annual report for his investment firm, Berkshire Hathaway, he noted:

"Most investors, both institutional and individual, will find that the best way to own common stocks is through an index fund that charges minimal fees. Those following this path are sure to beat the net results (after fees and expenses) delivered by the great majority of investment professionals."[24]

In the next chapter, I'll discuss what is probably one of the most talked about subjects in the investment world but also one of the least understood; how you should allocate your investment dollars. And I'll show how several often-advised allocations would have done over 30-plus years.

Finally, an article in *The Wall Street Journal Sunday,* a former insert in many Sunday papers, entitled "Secrets of the 401(k) Millionaire," Jan. 15, 2012, noted one common characteristic among the 0.2 percent of 401(k) participants who have saved more than $1 million.

"They don't necessarily have higher than average salaries or the investing IQ of Warren Buffett," said Jack VanDerhal, *research director at the Employee Benefit Research Institute* (in Washington, D.C.)

"The one characteristic that differentiates the winners from the non-winners here is contribution rate—a high percentage of those million-dollar savers had constant participation and high contribution rates."[25]

In other words, **they saved as much as they could for as long as they could**—and I'll bet **they started saving as soon as they could**.

Chapter 10

Spread your eggs around

Asset allocation reduces risk, boosts investment returns

I once had a photography mentor who advised that I could know how to do a job but I'd never be the boss until I knew why I was doing it. Similarly with investing, I can tell you how to invest but you won't achieve any degree of mastery until you know why you're doing it. That's the purpose of this chapter on **asset allocation: to put your money in several investment types that hopefully won't go up and down at the same time or at the same rate.**

Asset allocation is probably most confusing for new investors, in part because investment advisors use confusing terms that aren't well-defined; they use different terms for similar concepts, and they don't agree much in their forecasts.

I've joked in my classes that you can listen to three different investment advisers and get five different opinions.

A first step to understanding asset allocation is to understand volatility. **To be volatile is to be "likely to shift quickly and unpredictably; unstable,"** says Webster's New World Dictionary, Third College Edition.[1]

Don't put all your eggs in one basket.

In this discussion, it refers to the stock market's short-term swings.

Simply put, **the larger the loss you face, the percentage gain you must achieve to get back to even grows even larger**.

You can check this out with a calculator: It takes just over an 11 percent gain to make up for a 10 percent loss. It takes a 25 percent gain to make up for a 20 percent loss, a 33.34 percent gain to make up for a 25 percent loss, and a 100 percent gain to make up for a 50 percent loss. When you reach a 90 percent loss, it takes a 900 percent gain to get back to even.

Therefore, **you want to avoid big losses as much as possible**.

The sidebar, "Volatility is a fact of life in the investing world," gives an example of volatility and provides historical examples.

The first way to avoid losses is to wait to invest in stocks or stock mutual funds until you have at least a five-year time horizon.

Statistics show that in about 80 percent of five-year periods, stocks have bested other investments.

For 10-year periods, it's around 95 percent.[2]

And for 15-year periods, it's 100 percent.[3]

Investments are for the long term.

You'll also want to allocate your investments to asset classes that don't all go up and down at the same time or at the same rate.

The goal of asset allocation is to protect your money during a market downturn by putting some of it into assets that will keep growing—or not go down as much—during such a period.

Volatility is a fact of life in the investing world

Suppose you want to invest $1,000 for two years. I offer you a choice of a bond that will yield 5 percent each year or a stock that I know will drop 10 percent in the first year but will jump 20 percent in the second year.

Which should you choose? A 20 percent return on a stock is pretty good but it's hard to first take a 10 percent loss. Or a 5 percent yearly return on a bond is not much but at least it's steady and moving in the right direction.

Or does it make any difference? Five percent plus 5 percent equals 10 percent, and a minus 10 percent plus 20 percent also equals10 percent.

This is a word math problem; the answer is found in doing the math:

	Bond	Stock
Initial investment	$1,000	$1,000
First year gain	(5%) $50	(-10%) -$100
Total after one year	$1,050	$900
Second year gain	(5%) $52.50	(20%) $180
Total after two years	$1,102.50	$1,080

The above example teaches that the short-term ups and downs in stock prices (called volatility) can cost one dearly.

This is the main reason anyone planning to invest for less than five years is advised not to invest in stocks or stock mutual funds. In the example above, it would take a 27-percent gain to make up for a 10-percent loss and beat a bond yielding 5 percent yearly.

But over the long run, stocks have had higher returns than bonds. Let's take our example one year further: The bond again yields 5 percent and the stock grows by 10 percent. The bond would then be worth $1,157.63 and the stock would be worth $1,188.

Several Wall Street terms denote downturns of increasing magnitude. They, and what they mean in mathematic terms, are described below:

Correction: A 10 percent decline in stock prices. Mathematically, this is pretty insignificant; it takes an 11.12 percent rise to get back to even.

Example: $100 − 10% = $90; $90 + 11.12% = $100.03.

Bear market: A 20-25 percent decline in stock prices. Mathematically, a 20-25 percent drop is harder to return from; a 20-percent drop requires a 25 percent rise, while a 25-percent drop requires a 33.34 percent rise.

Examples: $100 − 20% = $80; $80 + 25% = $100. $100 − 25% = $75; $75 + 33.34% = $100.

Great Recession: From its high in October 2007 to the bottom on March 9, 2009, the Standard & Poors 500 stock index fell 56.8 percent (my own portfolio dropped 48 percent). It took four years to recover. Mathematically, it takes a 126.25% gain to make up for a 56.8 percent loss.

Example: $100 − 50% = $50; $50 + 100% = $100.

Great Depression: From its pre-crash high on September 3, 1929, to the bottom on July 8, 1932, The Dow Jones Industrial Average fell 89 percent. It took 25 years for the Dow to recover, which it did on November 23, 1954. Mathematically, it takes a 900 percent gain to recover from a 90 percent loss.

Example: $100 − 90% = $10; $10 + 900% = $100.

Sources: Yardeni Research, Inc.,[4] Time[5]

Two allocations tested

I've put several asset allocation strategies to the test, seeing how they would have done against the actual results from 1990 through 2021 as shown in the Callan Periodic Table of Investment Returns[6], (www.callan.com/research/periodic/). The table (which looks like the periodic table hanging on the wall of your high school science class—hence the name—depicts the investment returns for ten asset classes, ranked from best to worst (top to bottom) over the latest 20-year period.

The table shows that the best asset class for one year may be the worst in the next. After a string of good years near the top, an asset class may be near the bottom for several years and vice versa.

The two graphs that accompany this chapter show how an all-stock allocation and a commonly advised 60 percent stocks, 40 percent bonds allocation would have done from 1990 through 2021, starting with an initial investment of $5,000.

As with the "volatility" example in the accompanying sidebar, if the Callan Periodic Table showed an asset class went up by 5 percent in a year, I added 5 percent to its total; if it went down by 10 percent, I deducted 10 percent.

All-stock allocation: A recommended all-stock allocation calls for putting 25 percent in a large-capitalization growth-and-income mutual fund, 25 percent in a large-cap growth fund, 25 percent in an aggressive growth fund and 25 percent in an international fund.[7]

The first graph, "$5,000 invested in an all-stock portfolio" estimates how that would have done with $5,000 invested, $1,250 each, in S&P 500 value stocks (selected to represent growth and income stocks), S&P 500 growth stocks, Russell 2000 Small Cap Index growth stocks (to approximate aggressive growth) and the MSCI EAFE International Index.

This allocation shows what you would have earned had your investments gotten the same return as these market averages; they would have yielded $89,813 by the end of 2021. The large-cap growth stocks did best over this 31-year period, earning $42,524. The large-cap value stocks were second, growing to $22,852. The small-cap growth stocks did third-best at $18,171. The international stocks index lagged behind the other three, growing to only $6,267.

Note that all four classes declined by varying degrees in the 2000-2002 downturn, and all dropped in the 2008 market crash.

The combined portfolio declined from $20,258 in 1999 to $11,674 at the end of 2002, then dropped from $23,186 in 2007 to $17,436 at the end of 2008.

60 percent stocks, 40 percent bonds: This commonly advised allocation strategy is based on an old rule of thumb that you should subtract your age from 100 to determine what percentage of your portfolio should be in stocks.[8] Or more simply, you should match the proportion of bonds in your portfolio to your age.

When you're younger, you should be heavily in stocks; as you get older, you should have more bonds in your portfolio.

Recently, writers have also advised subtracting your age from 110 or 120 to determine what percentage of stocks you should hold. Because we're living longer—and will need retirement income for longer—they advise holding more stocks later in life.[9]

I believe the 60-percent stocks, 40-percent bonds allocation is recommended so often because it's near the midpoint of this continuum. Or maybe people don't think about investing until middle age, and this is the recommendation that then fits their age.

I used the Callan Periodic Table to see how this allocation would have done, as is shown in the second graph, "$5,000 invested, 60% stocks, 40% bonds."

I was pleasantly surprised to discover that the bond portion, which consistently yielded around 6 to 9 percent yearly—and didn't suffer the market downturns of 2000-2002 and 2008-2009—made up for the declines in the S&P 500 Index, resulting in a $90,802 total by the end of 2021, which was $989 ahead of the all-stock allocation.

That's been unusual in the years I've been monitoring this allocation but it shows the benefit of hedging one's investments: holding an asset class that doesn't move in tandem with the stock market as a way to protect against financial loss.

In the 2002 and 2008 market downturns, the totals didn't drop as far as they did with the all-stock allocation. At the end of 2002, The stocks/bonds allocation was $3,899 ahead of the all-stock allocation; at the end of 2008, it was $1,370 ahead.

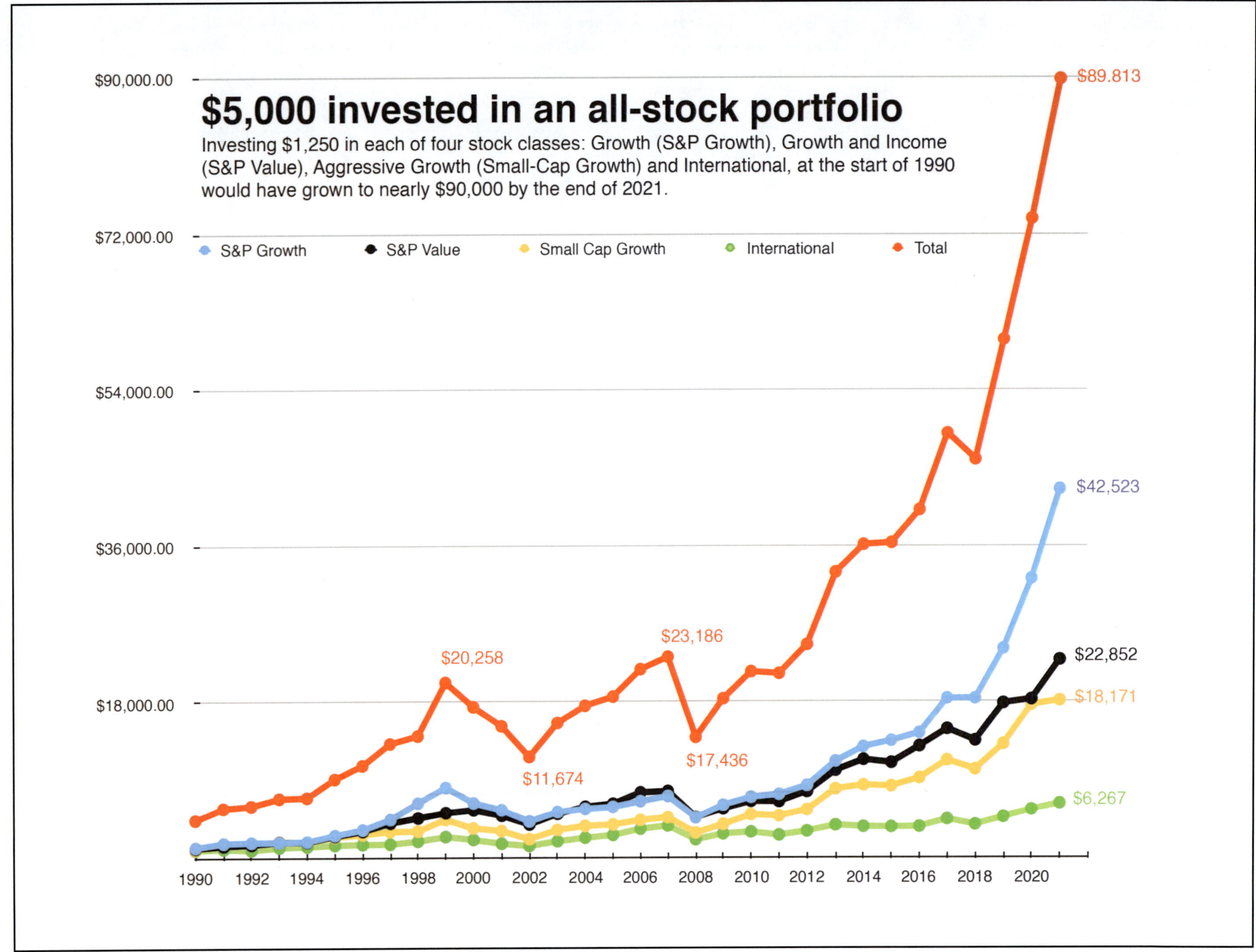

Type to enter a caption.

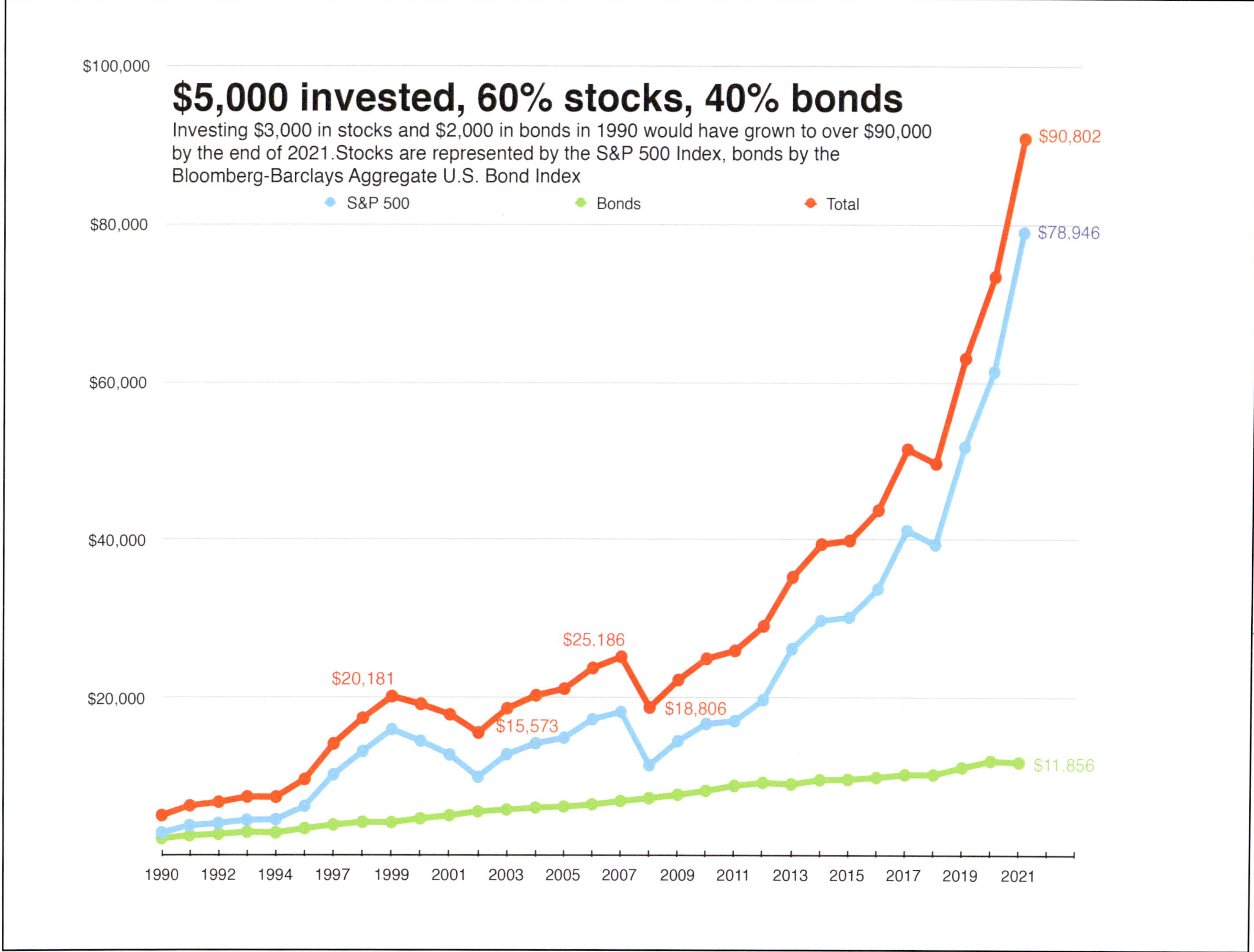

Type to enter a caption.

I believe this commonly advised allocation might be good in a workplace retirement plan because, as noted in the last chapter, around 70 percent of U.S. stock funds fail to outperform the S&P 500, and many 401(k) plans have an S&P 500 Index fund as an investment option. But it's doubtful that these plans would also offer the ever-changing 30 percent that outperform the index after costs are deducted.

However, an important caveat as of this writing in 2024: Invest only in an intermediate-term bond fund with maturities of no more than 3 to 5 years. That's because recent record-low interest rates are going up, and rising rates will lower the value of existing bonds. The sidebar "As interest rates rise, bonds fall in value" explains why.

Intermediate-term bond funds replace maturing bonds with new ones every day, so when interest rates rise, they will soon start buying new higher-yielding bonds, but it will still take three to five years before all the lower-yielding bonds cycle out.

A substitute for bonds

If you'd like to follow this strategy but don't want to invest in bonds during a rising interest rate environment, a balanced fund composed of bonds, income-producing stocks and perhaps cash equivalents, may be a good substitute.

Balanced funds contain a mixture of stocks and bonds, and perhaps money market funds. They are for investors who want safety, income and modest capital

As interest rates rise, bonds fall in value

Just like a seesaw, as interest rates rise, bond prices fall, and vice versa.

Let's say you buy a $1,000 10-year bond that yields 3 percent yearly. A year later, the interest rate rises to 4 percent. Your bond still yields 3 percent but if you now want to sell it, the price will be $925. A buyer will not want to pay $1,000 for a bond yielding 3 percent when he can now buy one yielding 4 percent. The new price will give him a 4 percent yield to maturity for the nine years left.

If the interest rate falls, bond prices rise. Rather than rising to 4 percent, let's say the interest rate falls from 3 percent to 2 percent. Now your $1,000 10-year bond is worth more because a buyer can no longer get one yielding 3 percent. So, your bond's price rises to $1,082, which would give the buyer a 2 percent yield to maturity for the nine years remaining.

Source: Securities and Exchange Commission[10]

appreciation, says Investopedia.[11]

Balanced funds generally contain about 60 percent income stocks and 40 percent bonds. Income stocks are typically those that have limited growth prospects but pay a steady, perhaps increasing dividend. A public utility stock is perhaps the classic stereotype of such a "widows and orphans" stock, so named because trust funds invest in them to provide for their beneficiaries.

A balanced fund should be found in a 401(k) plan and yield similarly to corporate bonds.[12]

Not much difference

One big takeaway from the above comparisons is that after 31 years, the amount earned from each of these portfolio allocations wasn't much different. Throughout the years that I've been making these comparisons, the all-stock allocation has bested the 60-percent S&P 500, 40-percent bonds allocation by about $1,500 in most years.

It has been unusual for the 60-percent S&P 500, 40-percent bonds allocation to beat the all-stock allocation.

For example, at the end of 2013, which was one of the best years in the stock market ever, the all-stock portfolio ended the year $1,600.96 ahead of the 60 percent S&P 500, 40 percent bonds allocation.

This is not to say that asset allocation isn't important. When investing larger sums of money, a small percentage difference can mean a lot in real money earned.

But you don't need to be concerned until you have around $50,000 or more to invest.

A second big takeaway from the graphs is that you can protect yourself from market downturns by investing part of your portfolio in non-stock market assets, such as in an intermediate bond fund or a balanced fund, without greatly affecting your returns.

That's good to know if you have a low risk tolerance or you're getting older.

Consider your risk tolerance

When you have a long time before you'll need the money, there's nothing wrong with seeking strong growth through an all-stock portfolio; you'll have plenty of time to weather downturns.

Nor do you then want all your money in relatively safe but low-yielding assets such as bonds, even if you're a scaredy-cat by nature.

On the other hand, if you're in or near retirement, you'll want to have much—if not most—of your money in safer assets than stocks to protect yourself from a downturn like we saw in 2008-2009.

You don't want to then have an all-stock portfolio, even if your personality is that of a high-stakes gambler.

To help you better understand your personal risk tolerance, Rutgers University has an Investment Risk Tolerance Quiz in pdf format that you can download for free. Google Rutgers Investment Risk Tolerance Quiz or go to http://njaes.rutgers.edu/money/assessment-tools/investment-risk-tolerance-quiz.pdf.[13]

Conclusion

As the above examples show, there wasn't much difference resulting from investing $5,000 in these two sample asset allocations.

Choose one that works for you, based on the time you'll have the money invested, your personal risk tolerance and the quality of the mutual funds inside your tax-advantaged plan at work, if that's the primary investment vehicle you're using.

If you are investing at work, seek the advice of your plan sponsor on how to allocate your investment dollars.

If you are investing on your own outside of work, seek out an investment adviser who will take an interest in your situation and will explain his recommendations so that you understand them.

And learn about investments so you better understand them and can discuss them with your plan sponsor at work or your investment adviser. Common terms are described in the accompanying sidebar.

Investor Protection Trust also provides free information about various investments: www.investorprotection.org/learn-about-investing/ or write to Investor Protection Trust, 919 Eighteenth Street NW, Suite 300, Washington D.C. 20006-5517.[14]

Mutual funds, other terms described

Growth funds invest in companies that are growing rapidly. They reinvest most of their profits for research and development rather than to pay dividends. They try to generate capital gains rather than income.

Growth-and-income funds seek both capital appreciation and income through dividends or interest payments. Favored by investors with moderate risk tolerance, they seek stability and to outpace inflation.

Income funds emphasize current income, on a monthly or quarterly basis. They usually hold a variety of government, municipal and corporate debt obligations, money market instruments and dividend-paying stocks, especially those with long histories of paying dividends, such as utility stocks, blue-chip stocks or preferred stocks.

Balanced funds contain a mixture of stocks and bonds, and perhaps money market funds. They are geared for investors who want safety, income and modest capital appreciation.

Value funds invest in companies deemed to be underpriced. They expect to make money by buying stocks before their expected upturn. These are often stocks of mature companies that have stopped growing and use their earnings to pay dividends.

Small-, mid- and large-cap stocks have different size market capitalizations: stock price times number of shares outstanding. There are no agreed-upon dividing lines but they perform differently. Small-cap stocks are younger, riskier firms that can shoot up in value and fall just as fast. Mid-caps, larger and more stable, provide more steady growth. Large-caps, well-established firms, provide growth but mainly income.

Stock market indexes measure the value of a part of the stock market and are used to describe the market as a whole or to compare the index's performance with individual stocks. An index is computed from the prices of its stocks (typically a weighted average). The S&P 500 Index comprises large and mid-cap stocks; the Russell 2000, small-cap stocks; the Wilshire 5000, nearly every U.S. publicly traded firm.

Index funds invest in all the stocks measured by a particular market index. An index fund provides broad market exposure, low operating expenses and low portfolio turnover.

"Indexing" is a form of investing that has outperformed most actively managed funds due to index funds' low costs. Managers merely replicate the performance of an index and, therefore, don't need research analysts and others who assist in the stock selection process. Also, they don't incur the costs of buying and selling stocks like actively managed funds.

Sources: Investopedia.com,[15] InvestorWords.com,[16] Wikipedia.com[17]

This art deco gas station/cafe in Shamrock, Texas, depicted in the movie *Cars*, is a popular stop along historic U. S. Route 66.

Retire to do what you want to do

Just make sure you are able to make your dreams come true

When I retired in October, 2012, I celebrated by taking a trip out West. Firing up my 1997 Ford Mustang Cobra, I took a bucket-list trip along parts of old U.S. Route 66 to California, a trip down memory lane for me.

That's because when I was young, my older brother, Milo, had settled there after leaving the U.S. Navy. My folks made a trip to visit him every couple years. Being a car fan, and having grown up on Westerns, I love the West and the roadside culture of the '50s and '60s.

Starting in Springfield, Mo., I meandered southwestwardly through a corner of Kansas and Oklahoma, where I stopped to visit my brother's second child, Lisa, who lives near Oklahoma City. From there, I crossed the Texas panhandle, where I visited the art deco service station made famous in *Cars*.

In New Mexico, I went to Santa Fe to see the Loretto Chapel with its miraculous spiral staircase that seems to have no means of support. After leaving Old Town Albuquerque, I was off to Arizona, where I stayed in Holbrook, home to the famous Wigwam Motel.

I'd always wanted to see the Painted Desert and Petrified Forest, which I did the next day before standing on the corner in Winslow made famous by the Eagles in *Take it Easy*, traveling through Flagstaff and marveling at a Grand Canyon sunset.

Following the original U.S. 66 route through Seligman, I overnighted in Kingman and had breakfast at a small-town café in Oatman, not far from the California border. That afternoon I reached my brother's house, where I stayed for three days.

It was a bittersweet trip; he had Parkinson's disease, and I was able to spend time with him before he died. He was 80.

That trip, in microcosm, is what retirement means to me, to be able to do what I've always wanted to do but that the pressures of work wouldn't allow, and being with the ones I love while I still can.

You, of course, have your own retirement dreams. And hopefully, by the time you're ready to retire you'll be able to accomplish them.

But you still need to manage your money so you'll have enough to last throughout your life and/or leave an inheritance.

That means you need a portfolio allocation that provides you with income, protects your accumulated wealth and grows enough to stay ahead of inflation. It also helps to keep taxes at bay.

More conservative allocations

Assuming that you follow the advice given in previous chapters, you'll have a sizable investment portfolio as you approach retirement, perhaps allocated about 60 percent to stocks, 40 percent to bonds and/or other assets that don't necessarily fluctuate with the stock market.

Many advisers say that this is the proper proportion for a middle-aged investor, depending upon his or her risk tolerance. Vanguard founder Jack Bogle suggested that an easy rule of thumb for asset allocation is to have your age invested in bonds and like assets.[1] A person in their 20s might have 80 percent in stocks, 20 percent in bonds; a person in their 30s, 70 percent stocks, 30 percent bonds.

As stated earlier, young people have 30 to 40 years to go before they retire, plenty of time to recover from market downturns. So they don't need the floor that bonds provide to an investment portfolio.

On the other hand, someone in their 50s is approaching retirement and wouldn't want to see a portfolio's value drop by over 40 percent, like I saw mine do—when I was 58—during the crash of 2008-2009.

As you approach retirement with a sizable portfolio, you'll want to protect it as well as continue to grow it in order to stay ahead of

"Standing on a corner in Winslow, Arizona," from the Eagles' *Take it Easy*, is memorialized in that city.

inflation and taxes, the real threats to your portfolio at this age.

That's why many advisers recommend that persons approaching retirement go from a 60 percent stocks, 40 percent bonds allocation to

Grand Canyon visitors climb out onto an outcropping to enjoy late afternoon light illuminating the rock formations.

"I alone know the plans I have for you, plans to bring you prosperity and not disaster, plans to bring about the future you hope for."

— JEREMIAH 29:11, GOOD NEWS BIBLE: TODAY'S ENGLISH VERSION

a 50/50 split, or a 40 percent stocks, 60 percent bonds allocation. As noted in the asset allocation chapter, you may give up a little return in exchange for some downside protection. As you acquire a sizable portfolio, that exchange can be worth it.

Therefore, as you get into your 70s and 80s, you'll probably want to move to 30 percent stocks, 70 percent bonds, or 20 percent stocks, 80 percent bonds, as you have fewer future needs and more current needs, perhaps due to illness or incapacity.

Some investment advisors, such as Adam Bold, founder of the Mutual Funds Store and the Mutual Funds Show, have recommended putting retirement money into two pools, an income pool from which you'll draw money for living expenses, and a growth pool, which will continue to accumulate for future wants and keep you ahead of inflation.[2]

Creating two investment pools makes sense to me because they have different time horizons: the income pool will be assessed yearly and should have conservative investments like bonds and dividend paying stocks, while the growth portfolio won't be touched for at least five years, and can be invested in riskier but more rewarding growth stocks.

Control your withdrawals

A strategy for taking withdrawals that's been widely quoted is the Four-Percent Rule. It says that you should be able to withdraw 4 percent of your investments yearly and not run out of money over a 30-year retirement.[3]

So if you have accumulated $1 million by retirement, you should be able to take out $40,000 annually and still earn enough on your remaining balance that you don't run out of money before you die.

However with current low rates of return as of this writing, many advisors say 4 percent may be too rich; you may not be able to maintain that throughout retirement.

I'm conservative; I suggest 4 percent should be an upper end to withdrawals, used in good times.

The bottom line is that you need to continue budgeting, just like you did when you were saving for retirement, taking just enough to live well, and keeping the rest invested for the future.

Personally, I take just enough from my income pool each month to cover living expenses that aren't met by Social Security. As you'll remember from the budgeting chapter, Social Security meets most of my fixed living expenses, so how much I withdraw from my portfolio to an extent depends upon what I need to meet occasional or unexpected expenses or how high on the hog I want to live that month.

Minimize your taxes

Dr. Thomas J. Stanley, writing in *The Millionaire Next Door* and his subsequent books, also noted that one of the principal characteristics of self-made millionaires is that they are good at minimizing their realized income while maximizing their unrealized income.[4] That means most of their

investments are in assets like real estate and stocks or mutual funds that don't generate taxable cash flows. They structure their portfolio so their realized taxable income is quite small in comparison to their net worth.

My retirement strategy perhaps puts this most simply. I have two pools of money, the first of which came from my share of the proceeds from the sale of the newspaper company, which is taxable money.

The second pool of money is made up of my 401(k) and Roth IRA contributions. As I've been able to—through two job changes, one change in business ownership, and after turning 59-1/2—I've rolled over my 401(k) proceeds into a Roth IRA, as well as made my own yearly Roth IRA maximum contributions. This money provides a good vehicle for growth because it grows tax-free.

I take just enough from the first pool to stay within the 10 percent tax bracket.

If I should need or want to spend beyond the 10 percent bracket—such as for a new car, an expensive vacation or to pay medical bills, I first have my emergency fund, which is now about a year's worth of expenses beyond what Social Security will meet. Then I would pull from my Roth IRA proceeds, which can be withdrawn tax-free.

Other considerations

Preparing for retirement and living well in retirement could be a book by itself but here are a few more things to consider.

• **Buy long-term care insurance once you turn 60:** Statistically, if one makes it to age 60, one has a very good chance of living into old age and needing nursing home care.[5] This is especially important if one wants to leave money to a spouse or children; otherwise, a large part of your estate may have to go toward long-term care.

• **Choose when to retire:** About 40 percent of workers retire at age 62, when they can first take Social Security, according to the Social Security Administration. That rises to near 50 percent before workers reach Social Security's full retirement age.[6]

I, too, retired at 62 because I didn't like the job I had at the time, I wanted to do other things and, fortunately, I had a large enough portfolio that I could do so. In fact, I believed I could invest my Social Security benefit (actually, a like amount) and make more on it than I could by waiting for a larger benefit.

If you have health issues, you also may want to consider taking benefits early.

But if you're in good health, you like your job—and especially if you haven't built enough wealth to retire—plan to work a few more years. That will help you in two ways.

Working more years allows you to contribute more to your retirement investments, growing them further before you retire. Secondly, postponing Social Security will cause your benefit to grow yearly until age 70. From your full retirement age to age 70, your benefit will grow by 8 percent yearly, which is not a bad return.

• **Choose when to take Social Security:** This goes along with the point above. There are many strategies for how a couple can claim Social Security, too many to go into here. What's best for you and your spouse will depend upon your individual situation. Contact a professional for guidance before you claim Social Security benefits.

Maria Bruno, Vanguard's head of U.S. wealth planning research, likened Social Security to an annuity to be paid out over the rest of your life: Waiting to take it can be a hedge against running out of money.[7]

Based on Bruno's comment, it struck me that it *might* pay for a wife to postpone taking her benefit as long as she can. Women statistically outlive their husbands, and she may bear the costs of his final care and funeral expenses, which could eat up a big portion of their savings. Thus taking Social Security later could give her a much-increased benefit through the end of her life.

But again, when couples should claim Social Security will depend upon their individual situation; consult a professional before taking any action.

• **Create or update a will:** At least, decide who you want to inherit your property and appoint a guardian for young children.

You may also want to create a living trust, which is becoming popular to avoid the costly and time-consuming process of probate.[8] You also avoid the cost of probate with Pay on Death Bank Accounts and Transfer on Death vehicle titles, investment accounts and real estate deeds.[9]

You should also create a "living will," spelling out what medical care you do or do not want to receive if you're incapacitated.

Along with that, you'll need a "durable power of attorney for health care decisions," designating someone to make health care decisions for you if you can't. Preferably, that person should live nearby.[10]

You may also want a Do Not Resuscitate (DNR) order if you don't want to receive CPR or other resuscitation techniques if you stop breathing or your heart stops beating.[11]

You can also create a "durable power of attorney for finances," designating someone to manage your finances if you can't.[12]

These documents can be created with help from NOLO, a firm which provides free legal help to individuals and small businesses.[13] See www.nolo.com for more information.

• **Make sure your list of beneficiaries is up-to-date:** This is especially important with insurance policies, mutual funds and retirement accounts. The list of beneficiaries on those will supersede what's in your will.[14]

It is a common mistake for the deceased to have changed his/her will but to have forgotten to change an insurance policy or 401(k) plan started years ago. If he lists an ex-wife as his beneficiary, she will get that money, not his current spouse.

Make sure your list of beneficiaries is up-to-date after any of these life events: an adoption, birth of a child or grandchild, divorce, marriage, death of a beneficiary or any other situation where you would want to add or subtract one. You may want to include contingency beneficiaries should something happen to a primary beneficiary.[15]

CHAPTER 12

Your goal is freedom

Wealth allows you to do whatever you want to do

One Sunday late in 2006, I attended a Sunday brunch sponsored by the singles group of which I was a member. I sat next to a friend, Donna, who related that she and several of her girlfriends, who had a longstanding tradition of going to the beach for a week each September, had been to a travel show the day before and decided they wanted to do something different in 2007. They were organizing a trip to Alaska.

I commented casually that that was the way I'd like to travel — to go with a group of friends. I didn't think any more about it but by the time I got home that afternoon, I had an email message waiting for me, which had been sent by the organizers to all those tentatively planning to go.

It was an implicit invitation for me to join them; they even had already paired me with another man to share a cabin.

Afterward, I mused that many people receiving such an email would sigh, wishing they could afford to go on such an excursion.

Others would scrimp and save, perhaps working overtime or a second job, in order to raise the money to be able to go.

Roaring Fork Motor Nature Trail winds through the Great Smoky Mountains.

"There is one thing that gives radiance to everything. It is the idea of something around the corner."

— G. K. CHESTERTON

Still others might go into debt to pay for the trip and return to face years of paying for what was 12 days of fun.

I did none of those; when I saw the email, I exclaimed, "Hell yes, I'm going!"

And a group of 18 landed in Fairbanks in August 2007. After touring that city for a day, we took a train to Denali National Park, where we took a bus into the park's interior.

From there we traveled to Talkeetna, a town just below Denali, which was the inspiration for "Northern Exposure," and

A two-masted schooner sails down New York City's East River at sunset.

which is where many treks to climb Denali begin.

We then ventured down to Anchorage and Whittier, where we boarded the Diamond Princess and cruised Glacier Bay before heading down the coast, making ports of call at Skagway, Juneau and Ketchikan before ending our voyage in Vancouver, British Columbia.

We had a blast.

The goal of the journey we've been on through these pages is financial freedom, the ability to do whatever you'd like to do.

That includes pursuing the items on the bucket list you made after reading the goal-setting chapter as well as taking advantage of opportunities that come your way, like my Alaska trip.

Pursuing God's purposes

Financial well-being doesn't just apply to material goods or experiences you'd like to pursue. It also frees you to pursue the purposes God has for you.

As I neared retirement, I pondered, and fretted—as I'm sure many people do—over what I would do for the rest of my life. I was ready to leave that job but I wasn't ready to stop trying to make a difference in the world.

As with other times when I've changed careers, I looked to books on how best to do so. One of the best I came across was *What Color is Your Parachute? A Practical Manual for Job-hunters and Career-changers*, by Richard N. Bowles.

Inside, I found a "flower" exercise to be completed over several days, which was designed to clarify one's God-given purposes in life. The premise of the exercise is that by getting to better know yourself and your purposes in life, you'll make better vocational choices.[1]

Through that exercise, I concluded He wants me to pursue the following three purposes:
- Justice and morality,
- Love of God and country,
- Knowledge, truth and clarity.

And as anyone writing a mission statement for themselves or their company knows, it's best to create a simple, memorable phrase that sums up everything. In my case, that is summed up in the old

Superman theme: pursuing "truth, justice and the American way". I figure God is implied in "truth" and "justice."

As I shared this with a spiritual mentor, she wisely advised that these purposes also need to be tempered with mercy.

Continue your quest with these books

On life: (You should have read this in high school or college)

Covey, Steven R., *The Seven Habits of Highly Effective People,* New York, N.Y., Simon and Schuster, 1989

On economics: (An easy read; it explains economic principles well)

Sowell, Thomas, *Basic Economics: A Citizen's Guide to the Economy,* New York, N.Y. Basic Books, 2001

On living like real millionaires: (Dr. Stanley has surveyed them)

Stanley, Thomas J. and Danko, William D., *The Millionaire Next Door,* Atlanta, Ga., Longstreet Press, 1996

Stanley, Thomas J., *The Millionaire Mind,* Kansas City, Mo., Andrews McMeel Publishing, 2000

Stanley, Thomas J., *Millionaire Women Next Door*, Andrews McMeel Publishing, 2004

Stanley, Thomas J., *Stop Acting Rich: And Start Living Like a Real Millionaire,* Hoboken, N.J., Wiley 2009

On changing careers: (practical guides on knowing yourself and finding a career)

Acuff, Jon, *Quitter: Closing the Gap Between Your Day Job and Your Dream Job,* Brentwood, Tenn., Lampo Press, 2011

Bolles, Richard N., *What Color is Your Parachute: A Practical Manual for Job-Hunters and Career-Changers*, 2015 edition, Berkeley, Ten-Speed Press, 2014

On investing (the first is an easy read; the second harder but a great resource)

Murray, Nicholas. *Simple Wealth, Inevitable Wealth.* Mattituck, N.Y. The Nick Murray Company, 1999

Bogle, John C. *Common Sense on Mutual Funds: New Perspectives for the Intelligent Investor,* New York, N.Y., John Wiley and Sons, Inc., 1999 (updated in 2009)

And as I think about what to do in retirement, I thereby have a standard by which to judge the activities I ponder participating in. Do they serve "truth, justice and the American way?" If not, I know they're not worth my time.

All in all, it's a great book, and I highly recommend it to anyone seeking to clarify their career or life choices.

Writing this book was one of the "bucket list" choices that evolved from that introspection. Through it, I hope to serve those purposes as well as use the knowledge and talents I've acquired over the years.

Wealth is a tool

Dave Ramsey, in a recent edition of Financial Peace University, tells the story of a man worth $20 million, who was sitting in church with his wife when they noticed a young woman at the end of the pew, crying.[2]

The man nudged his wife, urging her to slide down, ask the woman what was wrong and if they could pray for her. They found out that she was a single mother; she was crying because she couldn't pay her electric bill, and the power was about to be cut off. They prayed with her and asked for her name and address, ostensibly to follow up with her.

But the next day, this multimillionaire went to the power company and anonymously paid the young woman's bill for a year in advance.

It would seem like a miracle to her, and in a sense it was, Ramsey said, that she encountered a multimillionaire who would use his money in this way.

Ramsey noted one must have some wealth to engage in this kind of charitable activity; if you're struggling to pay your own light bill, you don't have thoughts of helping someone else pay theirs. But after you've built wealth and know that your family, and grandchildren are taken care of, your wealth becomes a tool to help others.

Just a step

As I conclude, I leave you with a list of books that have helped me in my journey to prosperity. Just as there are no "get rich quick" schemes, there's no one resource that can help you become prosperous and happy. **Success—however you define it—is not a destination; it is a journey.**

This book hopefully has inspired you to think about what success in life means to you and how to go about achieving it.

If I can do it, you can too.

But this book is not the end of what you need to know to achieve your own success; this is just the beginning of your journey to prosperity. Use the resources listed in this chapter, or seek out other resources.

There's no definitive list to follow but I suggest starting with Steven Covey's *The Seven Habits of Highly Effective People*. It can probably be found in most public libraries. If there were a high school or college course called Life 101, aimed at preparing young people to go out into the world—and I think there should be—this would be the textbook.

Many people don't seem to get past the first habit: being proactive: making things happen by working to expand their "circle of influence" and not just complaining about the injustices they see in their lives as many people do.[3]

The second habit is "start with the end in mind." This is like the bucket list I gave you in the goal-setting chapter but is much more inclusive. The book offers an exercise where you are asked to imagine looking on at your own funeral and thinking about what you would want your spouse, family, friends and business associates to say in your eulogy.[4]

It's the ultimate goal-setting exercise and will hopefully steer you toward being the person that you want to be.

Beyond *The Seven Habits of Highly Effective People*, I'd recommend the *Millionaire Next Door* series. As I've noted in earlier chapters, this series documents who the real millionaires are in America, how they think and how they live. They're not like those portrayed on TV or in the movies.

And for a step-by-step program on how to get out of debt, save and invest to secure your financial future, take Dave Ramsey's Financial Peace University course. If one isn't offered near you, you can start one.

These resources can help you pursue your own financial dreams but like the pioneers, you'll have to forge your own path. Completing this book is just a step along the way. I hope it will encourage you to continue on your own life's journey to prosperity.

Bon voyage!

A van smashes through a roadblock for visitors at Universal Studios in California in the mid-1980s.

"The U.S. Constitution doesn't guarantee happiness, only the pursuit of it. You have to catch up with it yourself."

— BENJAMIN FRANKLIN

ENDNOTES

Chapter 1

[1]Stanley, Thomas J., and Danko, William H., The Millionaire Next Door, (Marietta, Ga. Longstreet Press Inc., 1996) 1–2.

[2]Ibid, 3–4

[3]Ibid, 12

[4]Ibid, 12–14

[5]"Albert Einstein – Compound Interest," Quotes on Finance, 12 February 2014, http://www.quotesonfinance.com/quote/79/Albert-Einstein-Compound-interest,

Chapter 2

[1]Stanley, Danko, 3

[2]James, Ali, "Back to School Thrifting," Knoxville News-Sentinel, July 30, 2013, 1D

[3]Ibid

[4]Ramsey, Dave, "Dumping Debt: Breaking the Chains of Debt," Dave Ramsey's Financial Peace University DVD series, (2008)

[5]Stanley, Danko, 29

[6]Ibid, 37

Chapter 3

[1]Ramsey, Dave, The Total Money Makeover: A Proven Plan for Financial Fitness, (Nashville, Tenn. Thomas Nelson Inc. 2007) 102

[2]Ibid, 104

[3]"Average Credit Card Rates (APR) – 2016," Value Penguin, 4 November 2016, https://www.valuepenguin.com/average-credit-card-interest-rates

Chapter 4

[1]"The Bucket List." Wikipedia.org, 27 October 2016 https://en.wikipedia.org/wiki/The_Bucket_List

[2]Ramsey, Dave, The Total Money Makeover: A Proven Plan for Financial Fitness, (Nashville, Tenn. Thomas Nelson Inc. 2013) 137-138

[3]United States Jaycees, Personal Dynamics, (Tulsa, Okla. 1976) 15

[4]Ibid

[5]Kimberly Amadeo, "Fed Funds Rate History: Its Highs, Lows and Charts," 14 December 2022, The Balance, 16 January 2024 https://www.thebalancemoney.com/fed-funds-rate-history-highs-lows-3306135

Chapter 5

[1]Ramsey, Dave, "Super Savers," Financial Peace University DVD series (2008)

[2]"How my FICO Scores are calculated," My FICO, 6 December 2016, http://www.myfico.com/credit-education/whats-in-your-credit-score/

[3]Simon, Jeremy M., The FICO 5: The components that make up a FICO Credit Score, 10 April 2010, Yahoo Finance, 2 December 2016 http://finance.yahoo.com/news/pf_article_109347.html

[5]Collins, Brian, "FHA Turns to Manual Underwriting to Reach More Borrowers," 9 December 2013, National Mortgage News, 10 July 2017, https://www.nationalmortgagenews.com/news/fha-turns-to-manual-underwriting-to-reach-more-borrowers

Chapter 6

[1]Michigan Counseling Association, Recommended Monthly Budget Percentages, 1 December 2016 http://www.michigancounselingassociation.com/uploads/2/6/3/4/2634297/budget__financial_education.pdf

[2]Perry, Larry, The Self-Sufficient Woman, (Oak Ridge, Tenn. and Chelsea, Mich., Performance Press 1989) 57–65

Chapter 7

[1]Ramsey, Dave, The Total Money Makeover: A Proven Plan for Financial Fitness, 173

[2]Prescott, Andy, "Is a Biweekly Mortgage Plan a Good Idea?", 24 April 2015, Clark Howard, 26 December 2016 http://www.clark.com/biweekly-mortgage-plan-good-idea

[3]Ibid

Chapter 8

[1]Stanley, Thomas J., Millionaire Women Next Door, (Kansas City, Mo. Andrews McMeel Publishing, 2004) 237–245

[2]Ibid

[3]Ibid, 239

[4]Ibid, 244

[5]Ibid, 261–279

[6]Ibid, 271

[7]Ibid, 279

[8]Ibid, 275–276

[9]"The Marketing Concept," Internet Center for Management and Business Administration, Inc., 2002–2010, 30 December 2016, http://www.netmba.com/marketing/concept/

[10]Stanley, Thomas J., Millionaire Women Next Door, 269

[11]Ibid, 202

[12]Stanley, Thomas J., The Millionaire

Mind, (Kansas City, Mo. Andrews McMeel Publishing, 2000) 136

[13]Ibid, 136–139

Chapter 9
[1]Laise, Eleanor, "Five Ways to Fix Up Your 401(k) plan," Wall Street Journal Personal Finance section, Knoxville News Sentinel, 1 February 2009

[2]"401(k) limit increases to $23,000 for 2024, IRA limit rises to $7,000," Internal Revenue Service, 1 November 2023, https://www.irs.gov/newsroom/401k-limit-increases-to-23000-for-2024-ira-limit-rises-to-7000

[3]Voigt, Kevin, "SIMPLE IRA Contribution Limits for 2023-2024," NerdWallet, 2 November 2023, https://www.nerdwallet.com/article/investing/simple-ira-contribution-limits

[4]Internal Revenue Service, https://www.irs.gov/newsroom/401k-limit-increases-to-23000-for-2024-ira-limit-rises-to-7000

[5]Rhinehart, Charlene, CPA, "Get Pumped: 2024 Roth IRA Income Ranges Have Increased," The Motley Fool, 27 December 2023, https://www.fool.com/retirement/2023/12/27/get-pumped-2024-roth-ira-income-ranges-have-increa/

[6]Laise, Eleanor, "Five Ways to Fix Up Your 401(k) plan."

[7]"S&P 500 – 10 Year Daily Chart," Macrotrends.nct, 17 July 2017, http://macrotrends.net/2488/sp500-10-year-daily-chart

[8]Ibid

[9]"How Much Should You Be Saving?" Vanguard, 4 January 2017, https://investor.vanguard.com/retirement/savings/how-much-to-save

[10]Ramsey, Dave, Dave Ramsey's Financial Peace University, (Brentwood, Tenn.: The Lampo Group, Inc., 2006) 153

[11]"Name the Top 7 Benefits of 529 Plans," 18 November 2013, Savingforcollege.com, 21 May 2014, http://www.savingforcollege.com/intro_to_529s/name-the-top-7-benefits-of-529-plsns.php

[12]"Compare savings options," 18 November 2013, Savingforcollege.com, 21 May 2014, http://www.savingforcollege.com/compare_savings_options/

[13]Weiss, Michael, "The Lowdown on No-Load Mutual Funds," 25 August, 2021, Investopedia, 23 January 2024, https://www.investopedia.com/articles/mutualfund/07/no-load.asp#:~:text=Key%20Takeaways&text=No%2Dload%20mutual%20funds%20have.funds%20outperform%20load%20mutual%20funds.

[14]Henricks, Mark, "Understanding Mutual Fund Expense Ratios, 20 May 2023, SmartAsset, 23 January 2024, https://smartasset.com/investing/mutual-fund-expense-ratio

[15]"Mutual Fund Fees and Expenses," U. S. Securities and Exchange Commission, 20 January 2024, https://www.investor.gov/introduction-investing/investing-basics/glossary/mutual-fund-fees-and-expenses

[16]Maverick, J. B., "What Is a Good Expense Ratio for Mutual Funds," 20 April 2021, Investopedia, 19 January 2024, https://www.investopedia.com/ask/answers/032715/when-expense-ratio-considered-high-and-when-it-considered-low.asp#:~:text=The%20average%20expense%20ratio%20for.typical%20ratio%20is%20about%200.2%25.

[17]Bogle, John C., Common Sense on Mutual Funds, (New York, N.Y., John Wiley & Sons, Inc., 1999) 402

[18]"See the Difference Low Cost Funds Can Make," Vanguard, 2022, 19 January 2024, https://investor.vanguard.com/investment-products/mutual-funds/low-cost?WT.srch=1&cmpgn=PS:RE

[19]Ibid

[20]Bogle, 92

[21]Bogle, 127

[22]Bogle, 127–128

[23]"Vanguard 500 Index Fund Admiral Shares" Vanguard, 2022, 29 April 2022, https://investor.vanguard.com/mutual-funds/profile/fees/vfiax

[24]Bogle, 118

[25]Olshan, Jeremy, "Secrets of the 401(k) Millionaires," SmartMoney.com, Wall Street Journal Sunday Personal Finance section, Knoxville News Sentinel, 15 January 2012

Chapter 10
[1]"Volatile," Def. 3a., Webster's New World Dictionary, 3rd College ed.1991, 1495.

[2]Shaw, Richard, "S&P 500 Safety over 5-year and 10-year periods," 8 October 2008, Seeking Alpha, 5 April 2017, https://seekingalpha.com/aticle/99066-s-and-p-500-safety-over-5-year-and-10-year-periods

[3]Ramsey, Dave, The Total Money Makeover: A Proven Plan for Financial Fitness, 145

[4]Yardeni, Edward; Abbott, Joe, and Quintana, Mali, "Market Briefing: S&P 500 Bull & Bear Markets & Corrections," 2017, Yardeni Research, May 31, 2017,

https://www.yardeni.com/pub/
sp500corrbear.pdf

[5]Suddath, Clair, "Brief History of The Crash of 1929," Oct. 29, 2008, Time, 25 July 2017, http://content.time.com/time/nation/article/0,8599,1854569,00.html

[6]"The Callan Periodic Table of Investment Returns," 2022, Callan Associates Inc., 2 May 2022, https://www.callan.com/research/the-callan-periodic-table-collection-year-end-2021/

[7]Ramsey, Dave, The Total Money Makeover: A Proven Plan for Financial Fitness, 146

[8]Ultimate Guide to Retirement: What's the Best Asset Allocation for My Age?" 2017, CNN Money, 25 April 2017, http://money.cnn.com/retirement/guide/investing_basics.moneymag/index7.htm

[9]Ibid

[10]"Interest Rate Risk — When Interest Rates Go Up, Prices of Fixed-Rate Bonds Fall," Securities and Exchange Commission Office of Investor Education and Advocacy, 1 May 2022, https://www.sec.gov/files/ib_interestraterisk.pdf

[11]"Balanced Fund," Investopedia, 25 July 2017, www.investopedia.com/terms/b/balancedfund.asp

[12]"What is a Balanced Fund?" The Motley Fool, 25 July 2017, https"//www.fool.com/knowledge-center/what-is-a-balanced-dund.aspx

[13]Grable, J.E., & Lytton, R.H., 1999, Financial risk tolerance revisited: The development of a risk assessment instrument, Financial Services Review, 8, 163-181. http://njaes.rutgers.edu/money/assessment-tools/investment-risk-tolerance-quiz.pdf.

[14]Investor Protection Trust, 2022, Learn About Investing, www.investorprotection.org/learn-about-investing/

[15]"Stock Fund," Wikipedia, 24 Much 2017, 2 May 2022, https://en.wikipedia.org/w/index.php?title=Stock_fund&oldid=771918518

[16]"Value Fund," InvestorWords.com, 2017, 25 July 2017, www.investorwords.com/5841/value_fund.html

[17]"Balanced Fund," Investopedia, 2017, 25 July 2017, www.investopedia.com/terms/b/balancedfund.asp

Chapter 11
[1] Bogle, John C., Bogle on Mutual Funds: New Perspectives for the Intelligent Investor, (Burr Ridge, Ill., and New York, N.Y., Richard D. Irwin, Inc. 1994) 239

[2]Bold, Adam, A Candid Session with Adam Bold, Feb. 14, 2014, The Mutual Fund Store. 22 March 2016 https://www.mutualfundstore.com/investing-insight/hot-topics-and-trends/february-2014-mid-quarter-mailbag-a-candid-session-with-adam-bold

[3]Holland, Kelley, "The 4 Percent Rule No Longer Applies for Most Retirees," April 22, 2015, CNBC, 22 March 2016 www.cnbc.com/2015/04/21/the-4-percent-rule-no-longer-applies-for-most-retirees.html

[4]Stanley, Danko, 55–60.

[5]Ramsey, Dave, Dave Ramsey's Financial Peace University, (Brentwood, Tenn.: The Lampo Group, Inc., 2006) 139

[6]Kroll, Melissa A. Z., and Olson, Anya, "Incentivizing Delayed Claiming of Social Security Retirement Benefits Before Reaching the Full Retirement Age," 2014, Social Security Bulletin, Vol. 74, No. 4, http://www.ssa.gov/policy/docs/ssb/v74n4/v74n7p21.html

[7]"Financial Advisors Swap Insights on Tough Client Questions, 26 October 2020, The New York Times, 6 February 2024 https://www.nytimes.com/paidpost/vanguard/financial-advisors-swap-insights-on-tough-client-questions.html

[8]Clifford, Denis, "Estate Planning Basics," 11th edition, (Berkeley, Calif., NOLO, February 2022), 16

[9]Ibid

[10]Ibid, 69–70

[11]Ibid, 74–75

[12]Ibid, 77–78

[13]Ibid, 18–21

[14]Ibid, 197–199

[15]Clifford, Denis, "Estate Planning Basics," (Berkeley, Calif., NOLO, August 2015), March 22, 2016) 18–21

Chapter 12
[1]Bowles, Richard N., What Color is Your Parachute? A Practical Manual for Job-Hunters and Career Changers 2016, (Bekeley, Calif. And New York, N.Y. Ten Speed Press 2016) 115–189

[2]Ramsey, Dave, "Retirement and College Planning: Mastering the Alphabet Soup of Investing," Dave Ramsey's Financial Peace University DVD series, (2008)

[3]Covey, Steven, The Seven Habits of Highly Effective People, (New York, N.Y., Simon and Schuster 1989) 66-94

[4]Ibid